THE A

THREE TEXTS BY AN EARLY ANARCHIST

ANSELME BELLEGARRIGUE

TRANSLATED BY

KIRK WATSON

2018

Contents

TRANSLATOR'S INTRODUCTION 6
TO ACTION!! AN INTERPRETATION OF THE DEMOCRATIC IDEA 10
    I. 12
    II. 14
    III. 17
    IV. 19
    V. 21
    VI. 24
    VII. 27
    VIII. 30
    IX. 34
    X. 36
    XI. 40
    XII. 43
    XIII. 47
    XIV. 50
    XV. 55
    XVI. 58
    XVII. 62
    XVIII. 64
    XIX. 66

XX.	70
XXI.	72
XXII.	76
XXIII.	79
MANIFESTO	**82**
ANARCHY IS ORDER	82
THAT THE TRADITIONAL COLLECTIVE REASON IS A FICTION	88
THAT THE INDIVIDUALISTIC DOGMA IS THE ONLY FRATERNAL DOGMA	93
THAT THE SOCIAL CONTRACT IS A MONSTROSITY	98
ON THE ATTITUDE OF THE PARTIES AND THEIR JOURNALS	103
POWER IS THE ENEMY	107
THAT THE PEOPLE ONLY WASTES ITS TIME AND PROLONGS ITS SUFFERINGS BY ESPOUSING THE QUARRELS OF THE GOVERNMENTS AND PARTIES	111
THAT THE PEOPLE CAN EXPECT NOTHING FROM ANY PARTY	116
ON THE POLITICAL ELECTORATE, OR UNIVERSAL SUFFRAGE	124
THAT THE ELECTORATE IS NOT AND CANNOT BE ANYTHING BUT A DUPERY AND A DESPOLIATION	129

PRIMOGENITURE AND THE FRENCH PEOPLE'S PORRIDGE 134

WHAT PRODUCES GOVERNMENTS IS NOT WHAT SUSTAINS THEM 138

TO UNMASK POLITICS IS TO KILL IT 145

CONCLUSION 151

THE REVOLUTION 153

I 153

II 157

III 161

IV 165

V 168

VI 173

VII 177

VIII 180

IX 183

X 186

XI 189

XII 192

XIII 195

XIV 198

THE ELECTORAL LAW 200

TRANSLATOR'S INTRODUCTION

A wise man neither lets himself be governed nor seeks to govern others: he wishes reason alone to govern, and for ever. --La Bruyère

Much like his German counterpart Max Stirner, the French thinker Jacques Marie Anselme Bellegarrigue (1813-~1870[1]) was an unappreciated genius who was promptly forgotten by his contemporaries, and only rediscovered and appreciated by later generations. Also like Stirner[2], he offered an early individualist philosophy which explicitly opposes the government to the individual. Unlike Stirner, though, he remains largely forgotten, even by most of his ideological fellow travelers in anarchist and libertarian circles.

His friend Ulysse Pic described him as "one of the most original minds you could ever meet"[3]. Bellegarrigue was a

---

[1] Michel Perraudeau-Delbreil, *Anselme Bellegarrigue, Le premier des libertaires*, p. 56.
[2] Stirner's *Der Einzige und Sein Eigentum* (*The Ego and Its Own*), published in 1844 preceded Bellegarrigue's writings by a few years, but which there is no reason to believe he read
[3] Ulysse Pic, *Lettres gauloises sur les hommes et les choses de la politique contemporaine*. A. Faure, 1865, p. XVII.

wanderer, having spent time in the United States before returning to France in time for the 1848 revolution, which forms the immediate subject matter of the writings translated here. In 1859[4], he left France for good, attracted by a position teaching law at the Universidad de El Salvador.

Bellegarrigue's political writings are few, brief, and easy to digest. They consist of a pamphlet, *To Action!! An Interpretation of the Democratic Idea* (1848), and two issues of his newspaper *L'Anarchie: Journal de l'Ordre* (1850): "Manifesto"[5] and "The Revolution".

Some of the salient concepts discussed in these writings which will be familiar from later writings in the anarchist, libertarian, and anarcho-capitalist schools of thought, such as: attacks on the social contract (which he calls "a monstrosity"), deregulation and decentralization, non-violent revolution, and refusal of support to the government. He considered the modern state a secularized continuation of the theocratic, monarchical state, which was kept alive by republican "schemers" who want to preserve its machinery but replace its staff.

A major issue of the day was the extension of universal (male) suffrage, and Bellegarrigue regarded centralized political democracy as sham democracy, as organized plunder, as necessarily producing the tyranny of a minority of voters who make a gift of their own freedoms and

---

[4] Perraudeau-Delbreil, ibid, pp. 47ff.
[5] Often published as "Anarchist Manifesto" or "Manifesto of Anarchy".

property, along with that of the non-voters, to their elected officials. The political opposition, along with the press that supports it, is nothing but the abettor of the ruling party's policies; by holding debates on any policy, they sanction its ultimate passage.

Bellegarrigue's analysis of the modern State reveals a violent, thieving, economically depressing organism. He called the slogan "tax the rich!" "the most senseless phrase that [had] been uttered" in his day. For him, labor and capital are natural counterparts, which eagerly cooperate in pursuit of their interests, when politicians don't interfere. He opposed welfare policies because they made the population dependent on the parties and government, instead of liberating themselves from it through productive economic activity and wealth.

On the constructive side of his ideology, Bellegarrigue starts out like Descartes with the basic recognition of the self, and constructs an ethics and politics upwards from there: one's own needs necessarily come first; by production and exchange with others, society comes together and the pursuit of individual interests turn to the good of the collective. He considers the town or municipality (*commune*) as the "complex individual", the natural social organism and the true home of human society and community; Murray Bookchin's libertarian municipalism[6] has a forerunner here.

---

[6] 3rd selection, section V and elsewhere in throughout these texts.

Although famous as an early anarchist, (a label he often uses for himself), Bellegarrigue is, strictly speaking, in the terms of contemporary libertarianism, a kind of minarchist[7]: his ideal nation would be self-governed at the municipal level, no municipality would govern any other; the only central institutions would be "an arbitration and a chancellery... an administrative commission, but not a government", along with a small ministry to handle international relations, and temporary ministries of war as needed.

Finally, Bellegarrigue presents a theory in which the individual will replace the state; for him, "the revolution is the emancipation of the individual or it is nothing", the end goal is "the substitution of the individual for the State". This is not an eschatological, idealistic, unrealizable notion, but something that can be practiced in everyday life when individuals simply reclaiming all the activities the State has usurped. Everyone can take matters into their own hands, creatively seeking productive outlets, earning a living according to luck and skill, making their own money and relying only on themselves.

---

[7] See below, *To Action...*: IX; *Manifesto*: "That the Social Contract Is a Monstrosity", and *The Revolution:* V.

TO ACTION!! AN INTERPRETATION OF THE DEMOCRATIC IDEA

1848

A people is always governed too much.
                                -Blair

They say I'm governed for my own good; and, since I must pay to be governed, it follows that I'm paying for my own good, which is possible; but still, it needs to be demonstrated.

Besides, since nobody knows how to make me happy better than me, I also find it strange, incomprehensible, anti-natural, non-human, to be devoted to the happiness of people one doesn't know; and I declare that I haven't had the honor of acquaintance with those who govern me.

It is only right, then, to say that, from my point of view, they really are too kind, and, ultimately, somewhat indiscrete, to be so concerned about my happiness, then, especially since it hasn't been shown that I'm incapable of pursuing it for myself.

In addition to this, devotion entails disinterestedness, and that these officious concerns can only be disruptive on condition that they're free of cost. I'm too well informed to quibble about questions of money, and may God keep me from questioning the devotion, and, by contrast, the disinterestedness of our statesmen. However, I beg permission to thank them until the delicate attentions with which they condescend to surround me, become less costly.

Toulouse, 1848.

I.

Had I a friend, just one friend — and, to have one, all I'd have needed is a good cook or a lovely woman, — I wouldn't have written what follows; it would have been something I shared with a confidant. Then, with the burden of my concerns lifted off my back, I would find solace from so many representative rigors in the fraternal arms of the bailiff.

But I have neither cook nor lovely woman; therefore, no friend, and, consequently, no confidant and so, for lack of anyone to talk to, I will speak to everyone. This way of keeping quiet will, I'm sure, be appreciated by the Republic.

And, as for the Republic, I humbly ask forgiveness to the lofty and almighty prose writers of *rue Lepelletier*, I take it upon myself to declare that this word — I've said, WORD — has begun to fatigue all of France, more than a little, from the Ocean to the Alps and from the Pyrenees to the Channel.

The words "the Republic" sits well upon its cadence of four syllables, but a word is not, after all, anything but a word, as a sound is only a sound; while a thing is a fact; and, the people, this is my belief anyway, lives more from facts than words.

If, then, we set aside ideas to discuss facts, I imagine such progress will be very much to the taste of all; when I say all,

I quite seriously mean to exclude from my formulation that polished class of citizens who follow what they read in *Le Moniteur*, that laborious congregation that condescends to pass its time pulling the budget by its tail, and without which we wouldn't know what to do, either with the public liberties, or the treasury's dollars.

I would like to know, — if God pleases, may I not be found too indiscreet! — I would like to know what is resolutely meant by "the Republic".

II.

A few months back, when agents were to be elected to proceed with the liquidation of the dead governments, those who had seen people without guardians, mature peoples; those who, too proud to be ambitious, made their democratic egoism consist in belonging to nobody else; those, finally, whose face had never been seen in the antechambers of any regime; the true democrats, the gentlemen of humanity, spoke of the Republic, and its name was not sullied upon their lips.

These men said, or they might have, concerning the members of the provisional government:

We can't expect the loquacious theoreticians to found democracy in France, to introduce freedom in practice and social reality.

There are great minds in the improvised council, but these great minds have kept intact both the governmental apparatus of the monarchies, and the administrative organism of the condemned constitutions; but these great intelligences didn't abrogate the organic legislation, which was based on the condemned constitutions; but these great intelligences have claimed all the power, the usurpation of which was the crime committed by the condemned constitutions.

They also said, or might have said:

Lamartine has written a Robespierréide *in which the autocratic principle of the* personification *of democracy is consecrated, and this doctrine will only stop being a poetic dream to become a Russian or Chinese style attack: — Judged!*

Ledru-Rollin plays the elitist as Guizot did before him: — Judged!

Louis Blanc is aristocratizing the workshops: — Judged!

All these men who say that France has won its liberties back effectively hold in their hands, and refuse to release, the liberties of France:

All these men who say that the people should govern itself really govern the people.

What we have here is dreamers or ambitious men, but not a single democrat.

And those who argued in this way expressed a very respectable opinion, for it was the opinion of France, of this France which desires only two simple and very legitimate things: to be free and to pay little.

In this epoch of which I've just spoken, an epoch that I will call republican since the authority was public, since all the citizens, instead of attaching to a government which existed only in name, attached themselves to the country, the only immutable fact, and felt the need to fraternally clasp each other's hands; in this epoch, I say, which preceded the meeting of the National Assembly, one could speak of the Republic: there were no parties then, there was only the party of common sense, the party of public morality based, in reality, on the democratic law of confidence in all, and sanctioned by the security of all.

Then, when one spoke of the Republic, everyone knew what it meant.

Today, when I uttered this word, I'm asked on all sides which color is the republic I'm talking about; and the mayor of my municipality (*commune*), who is only someone on condition of being something, as the prefect for authorization to have me arrested.

III.

We speak of a red Republic, we speak of a tricolor Republic, we speak of a moderate Republic, we speak of a violent Republic, we also speak of an Orléaniste, imperialist, even a Legitimist Republic.

Can we get an explanation of what this all means? For me, it's quite simple.

What it means is that the citizens called red are opposed to the exploitation of France by the tricolors, that the tricolors don't want it to be exploited by the reds, that the Orléanists, the imperialists, the legitimists oppose its exploitation by the reds and the tricolors. But that also means, to be fair, that both parties would be happy to assume the patriotic task of exploiting it, whether on their own account and officially, or *in extremis*, with a social rationale.

But, we shouldn't call wolves sheepfolds, and so I don't think we should call all these gentlemen Republics.

The Republic does not accept the crude absurdity of the official denominations listed above. There is only one republic of which I am, of which we are citizens, we honest folk, who don't aspire to anything, but who pay for the irreverent national domesticity. The Republic is us, it's the real France, exploitable and exploited material; the daily bread of all these fanatical Republics, of all these parties whose dream is the good of another and whose idol is idleness.

The Republic is to the parties as a tree is to parasites; the parties are the vermin of the nations, and it is important not to forget that it's to the various pretensions of these political religionists that we should march fitfully from revolutions to insurrections, and from insurrections to a state of siege, to periodically end in the burial of the dead, and in the payment of the revolutionary bills which are the prizes granted by the imbecility of all to the audacity of some.

Our forebears saw the France of the great vassals and that of the absolute kings; our fathers saw that of Marat, that of Danton, that of Robespierre, that of Barras, that of Bonaparte and that of Napoleon. We ourselves have seen the France of Louis XVIII, the France of Charles X, the France of Louis-Philippe, the France of the provisional government, the France of the National Assembly; but the France of nobody, that is, the France of everybody, the France of France, nobody has yet seen this, nobody, therefore, has seen the Republic; for the Republic is nothing other than the liberation of France from the tutelage of the governments.

IV.

Don't ask a democrat whether he's a socialist and of which sect; whether he's a conservative and of which sect; whether he's an Orléanist, an Imperialist, a Legitimist and of which sect. In the depths of all these social and political doctrines we can search for the free man and respect for the private funds, but all we'll find is paid masters and paying lackeys; but the democrat is not the kind who commands, since he's the one who refuses to obey.

If there are timid or servile people who seek shelter in Fourier[8], if there are some who lodge with Cabet or Proudhon, if some take refuge in Louis-Philippe, in Bonaparte, in Henri de Bourbon, I, for my part, declare that I can only reside with myself and that I offer nobody the renunciation of my identity.

How many yearn so strongly for the arrival of a supreme authority to whom all will bow! I proclaim my own arrival at actual sovereignty.

I'm not against the idea that, from gratitude, devotion or charity, some men may sacrifice a part of their time, their labor, their intelligence, their life, for the welfare of princes in need or ill-housed philosophers; everyone may give, as they like, alms of what he has to whoever he likes; and since, giving up on being oneself and acting for oneself, some are determined to live, think and produce for the

---

[8] Translator: "Fourrier" in the original.

benefit of dreamers, soldiers, or princes, let them have at it! The princes are poor and the dreamers even poorer than the princes; the dreamers are lazy and the princes are even lazier than the dreamers; the soldiers are vain and the dreamers are even more vain than the soldiers. But if they give themselves to the dreamers, to the soldiers or the princes, seizing for themselves the right to alienate, along with theirs, my time, my labor, my intelligence, my life, my liberty; if there is an obligation on my part to accept and pay the master who my neighbor takes for himself; if, by the mere fact that a dreamer, a soldier, or a prince has been installed at the Hôtel de Ville[9]; I'm obliged, on my part, to become the devoted servant of this dreamer, of this soldier, or of this prince, is beyond the limits of my comprehension.

If it's governing is thought to be a profession, I want to see the products made by this profession, and if these products do nothing for me, I declare that to force me to consume them is the strangest abuse of authority that one man can exercise over another. It is true that this abuse is exerted by force and that it's me who supports, with my money, this force I'm complaining of. With this in mind, thinking hard, I come to see that at the same time as I'm a victim, I'm also a fool.

But my foolishness comes from my isolation, and this is why I say to my fellow citizens: Lift your heads up; let's trust ourselves alone; let us say: *let there be liberty*, and liberty will be there.

---

[9] Translator: Something like the city hall, where the government was formed in Paris, February 1848.

V.

In this France of lofty seigneurs, princes, philosophers and generals; in this France, rebuked and whipped like a naughty child, by an unknown hand, for an unknown reason; in this France, in whose very center the governments have inoculated an administrative cancer of many billions, each *franc* of which is a ring on the chains that bind us; in this France, finally, where all is denied us, from the liberty of educating ourselves to the right of freely seasoning our food, each of us, as to what affects us, should shake out of their drowsiness and proclaim themselves minister for themselves, governor of their own France.

The France of each of us is the selfish and undeniable fact of our individuality with all that adheres to it: thought, production, results, property.

My France, my own, as a writer, is my thought, which I want to guide as an absolute ruler, the production of my thoughts is what I want control of; the result of this production which is mine alone to supervise, the property of the acquired outcome, which I wish to preserve and use at my own convenience and within the limits of the respect due to the thoughts, the production, the outcomes, the property of which everyone else's France is composed, no matter what, besides, their profession or their way of life.

Amid the infinite number of the diverse thoughts which are translated socially into the diverse products, thus, each producer necessarily has an instinct for the public's tastes; for the producer, who seeks consumers, isn't unaware that the latter only gives his money for a product that he likes and needs. The product can't be governed by someone who doesn't find his immediate interest in it, i.e., by the producer, without being upset and truncated; but if everyone governs their own thoughts, as a producer, then production will necessarily tend to a single goal: the satisfaction of the consumer, which is all of us; in the same way, if everyone governs their own thoughts as a consumer, a certain outcome is prepared for the results of the labor, and production will tend, in turn, to a single goal: the satisfaction of the producer, which is also all of us.

In this way, each is the beneficiary minister of all, and all are the beneficiary ministers of each, that is, that the producer benefits himself by benefitting the consumer, and the consumer gives comfort to his own existence while enriching the producer. And all this without effort, without anyone worrying about anything but their own interests, which necessarily spring from the interests of all. This is social harmony, in its democratic simplicity, which the Americans call, which practice, *self-government*.

Let me govern myself, and I can't disobey my instinct, which is to seek my own good; let me be governed, and I am sacrificed, since the instincts of my governor, who, subject to the same law as me, also seeks his own good, not only are not and cannot be mine, but also are and should be opposed to mine.

Let me thoughts be free, and I will produce, and my production will have an outcome and the outcome will bring me resources, the exchange of which will lead to me, and for my consumption, the products of others. If, on the other hand, my thinking is kept in check by an authority; if I am forbidden to state it in conformity with the infallible law of my instinct, and I don't produce or only produce badly; having no viable product, I can't perform any exchange. From which it follows that I won't consume; I am a burden to others and to myself: I am a spoke in a wheel that can't move.

Let's apply this isolated fact to everything, and we will find this swirling eddy of a social residue, unknown in the United States, but with which the governmental dikes have produced for France, this collection of stationary existences, which pass and return before the administration, like bodies floating on a compressed stream, constantly returning to the obstacle, and all we have now is a society where everything clashes and collides, or rather, a society that's immobile, banned, negated, cadaverized.

VI.

The organization of society is the slavery of individuals, and its disorganization leads to liberty, which unfolds upon the social body these rules of providential harmony, the observation of which, being in everyone's interest, ends up being universal among them.

But it's said that unrestrained liberty is threatening.

Who, then, does it threaten?

Who, then, should fear the untamed charger, but the man who's trying to tame it?

Who, then, is afraid of an avalanche, but the man who wants to halt it in its course?

Who, then, trembles in the face of liberty, but tyranny?

Liberty, threatening? The opposite is more like it. What's fearsome about it is the noise of its irons clanking. Once it's broken them, it is no longer tumultuous; it's calm and well behaved.

Let's not forget the order which followed the unfettering of 24 February, and above all, let's remember the disorder that followed the shackling of June!

The men of the Hôtel de Ville were then in government; that was their offense. They were nothing but the mere guardians of the seals set by the revolution upon the governmental succession of the royalty. We were the heirs of this succession; they thought it was them: — What folly! What was their dream? That they had their desired titles? That they were better than their defeated opponents? As if, in free nations, the government was a question of proper nouns! As if, in democracies, usurpation could argue for the integrity of the usurper!

That they were more capable? As if it were possible to have intelligence for everyone, when everyone keeps their own intelligence in reserve!

They should have noticed something quite simple, quite elementary, which is that, after divine right was relegated to the heart of the priesthood, nobody has received any mandate to act in the name of all and in the place of all.

But what was left undone by the provisional government, the Assembly could do; it might have been that this would democratize France; for, disregarding the mental dispositions of the great majority of the representatives, all that was needed was a single, truly democratic man, i.e., a man who had lived in the practice of democracy and liberty, to cast light on the situation and liberate the country. But this man, if he's about, has yet to show himself; nobody has spoken up in the tribune using the noble, disinterested, grandiose language of democracy. There are doubtless generous intentions in the Palais national; but unintelligent intentions are the abortions of human greatness, God's stillborn children, and the Assembly, like the provisional government, whose conduct it has sanctioned, misunderstood its mandate.

From its bosom we have seen the emergence of party men, theorists, political casuists, who have experience only of Monarchy, administrative elitism, the governmental management; men who have only ever seen liberty through the jealous veil of royalism.

Thus, we can say of the majority of the Assembly what we have said of the members of the provisional government: Let's not count on these theoreticians to establish democracy in France, to make freedom a reality in social practice.

VII.

The Representatives at the National Assembly were elected, as we shouldn't forget, to make a democratic constitution, i.e., to simplify the administration to the point that taxes are reduced and individuals are respected; they were elected to constitute the country.

What have they done, though?

Instead of constituting the country, they rushed to constitute themselves as governors; they deduced the conclusion before stating the principles; after which, and without unable to escape the dire precedents that they'd just established, they have been busy, as they had to be busied, with saving and preserving this government.

They have done this, and they have been consistent! Didn't the country, indeed, cease to exist the very day the Representatives met in the legislative palace? Didn't the assembly declare itself supreme, as absolute sovereign, notice! And so absolute, indeed, that it can do more than us, for it can act against us.

It can keep to its post indefinitely.

It can, by decree, have us incarcerated or outlawed, one by one or all at once.

It can sell France, one part at a time or all at once, to foreigners!

Someone will object that it won't do this; yes, and this is what remains of our hope, for I respond that it can do so; and I add that I don't understand how a free people can be regularly subjected to the discretion of a simple national representation which enjoys a modest instrument of action, composed of five hundred fifty thousand bayonets.

The national assembly only has the kings' intelligence; the democratic genius is alien to it.

The Assembly is a government; it was only meant to be a notary.

We have elected representatives to draft a contract to determine, in precise clauses, the ultimate line where the people ends and the administration begins: it has decided, without writing it, that the people ended everywhere and that the Government also began everywhere.

If the Assembly were the faithful expression of the national sovereignty, the laws or decrees that it gives would immediately apply to the safeguarding of the rights of the citizens, instead of applying only to its own security. The essence of the law is to express the will and protect the interests of all; for the law, everyone is supposed to keep it; well, let us examine all the decrees handed down by the Assembly: we won't find a single one that wasn't conceived in a view to preserve administrative immunities, by paralyzing the public liberties; we won't find a single one that doesn't consecrate fettering the social country in favor of the security of the official country.

VIII.

I don't believe in the efficacy of armed revolutions and I'll soon say why I don't believe in it. However, once a revolution of this sort is accomplished, once it is accepted, without contest, by the whole country, I see the possibility of turning it to the benefit of the nation.

What's the prerequisite for that?

Is the intervention of revolutionary action needed, does it need to be applied to the institutions?

The February Revolution, like that of 1830, only benefited a few men, since this Revolution, like that of 1830, abolished nothing but the proper nouns. Then, as today, the governmental machine kept, as it still does, the same machinery, and the only change I see is the hand that moving the handles.

What was meant when, on February 24, posters were pasted down the streets, and the papers printed that France had overturned the government and regained its liberties?

Did that only mean that the *National* had taken over from the *Journal des Débats*?

Did anyone grasp that the consequences of this event which shook the world, were limited to the victory of Marrast and his friends?

This, truly, would have been so much noise for such a minor task!

When the Revolution told us: "The French people has regained its liberties", we took the Revolution at its word and proclaimed in our hearts the abolition, not only of royalty, but of the royal government, of the government that clenched the liberties of France tight in its administrative talons.

Thus, by regaining our liberty of thought, the liberty of the press and the liberty of the vote, we have abolished, along with its budget, the government of the interior, which had been instituted to hold us in suspicion, for the benefit of the king's government.

Thus, by regaining our liberty to study, we have abolished, along with its budget, the government of public education, which had been instituted to suck our intelligence dry and to guide our education for the benefit of the king's government.

Thus, by regaining our liberty of conscience, we have abolished, along with its budget, the government of faith, which had been instituted to bring into the temple only those men whose influence was acquired in the interests of the king's government.

Thus, by regaining the liberty of trade, we have abolished, along with its budget, the government of commerce, which was instituted to incessantly keep the public credit under the thumb of the king's government.

Thus, by regaining the liberty of labor and industry, we have abolished, along with its budget, the government of public works, which was instituted to create large profits for the friends of the king's government.

Thus, by regaining the liberty of transactions and the liberty of the territory, we have abolished, along with its budget, the government of agriculture, which was instituted to hold the landowner, that is, he in whom the reason of the public's alimentation resides, directly dependent on the king's government.

Thus, by regaining the liberty to exist, we have abolished, along with its budget, the government of the barracks which, in peacetime, was only instituted to drive us into political nothingness, for the benefit of the king's government.

Thus, finally, by regaining all our liberties, we have abolished, with its multiple budgets, the complex administration of the bastard monarchies, this extortionate tutelage that was begotten in the stormy times of the imperial tyranny; which is dead, crushed by discussion, for over thirty years now, and whose rotten cadaver, for our lack of knowing where and how to bury it, asphyxiates our freedom.

If it's true that a Revolution abolishes something, look at what we abolished on February 24!

If it's true that the masses would engage in revolution to win their liberties, look at the liberties we won back on February 24!

IX.

The appeal to democracy made by the last Revolution was unheeded by our representatives.

At this appeal, faithfully interpreted, France might have leaped the fence and returned home, i.e., to the *commune*[10]. The nation, thus restored to its natural domicile, Paris was no longer anything but an inoffensive symbol, carrying out diplomacy with the world's nations, directing the navy, accepting or declaring war, on occasions and on stipulated conditions signing treaties of peace and trade, overseeing, internally, the execution of the laws, always simple and not numerous among a free people; naming, under its oversight, a minister of foreign affairs, a minister of justice, a minister of the navy and the colonies, a minister of war and an accountant, and doing its best with a budget that would have extended, in either a good or a bad year, except in case of hostilities and of paying interest on its debt, a figure ranging between four and five hundred million.

I'm not talking about the debt that stays beneath this combination. France can recognize the debt all the more when, returning to the *commune*, it regains possession of its own riches, which are relieved, by this single fact, of all the administrative charges that absorb the better part of its revenues. All I'm pointing to here is the liquidation of the royal government. I would force it, by axing seven budgets, to annually give back to the nation twelve hundred million

---

[10] I.e., "municipality", "village"; its people and officials.

francs at least, with which it could easily get rid of the debt in a few years.

But the most immediate benefit which France would see by abolishing these budgets is its liberty of action, the necessary consequence of which is the mutual confidence of its citizens, the end of the crisis, and the establishment of the national credit upon the ruins of this feverish governmental credit, a credit which is lit up or extinguished, as the government is stabilized or stumbles.

Outside of the ministerial departments of the navy and war, which are auxiliaries to that of foreign affairs, and, outside the grand judge, in whom the unity of the judiciary is represented, all the other departments are incompatible with public liberties, for they are only a carving up of the royal despotism, which kept all the elements of society under its thumb.

If trade, industry, education, religion, agriculture, if, in short, the French are free, then tell me what business do we have with the great masters of industry, trade, education, religion, agriculture, and the interior? Since when did Grand Masters ceased to be the sanction of servitude?

X.

Once the government of France is established on the foundations I've just laid, the parties will evaporate, ambitions will be extinguished, and the words Liberty, Equality, Fraternity will finally emerge from the domain of interpretations and controversies, entering the realm of facts.

I will explain myself, and my explanations will be simple.

What is it that actually resists the establishment of liberty, equality, fraternity among us? Ambition, i.e., the desire to dominate, to govern the people.

Where does ambition reside? In the parties; that is, in those who desire to dominate, to govern the people.

Where does a party find its *raison d'être*? In the certainty that, when victorious, it will be able to confiscate, for its own benefit, the national liberties and contributions; that is, in the possibility demonstrated to it that it could actually gain authority over all things, and thus impose itself on the people and its rival parties.

How can a party impose itself? By seizing the administration.

And what is the administration?

The administration is something abstract, indefinite, illogical, contradictory, obscure, incomprehensible, arbitrary, absurd, monstrous.

Something which derives neither from the heart, since it's arid and unfeeling; nor from science, since nobody understands any of it;

An instrument without form, without physiognomy and without proportions.

A noxious and cowardly myth, whose ruinous cult keeps a million priests occupied, who are no less insolent than fanatical.

A blind thing which sees all, deaf but which hears all, impotent but which can do anything, imponderable but all-crushing, invisible and filling everything, impalpable and touching everything, ungraspable and grasping all, inviolable and violating everything;

An incandescent nebulousness bringing lightning, thunder and asphyxia;

A magical, demonic and infernal invention that strikes, strikes, always strikes, on all occasions and in all directions, so that there is constantly, between its agents and the people, a rampart of twirling and whirling.

This is the administration! that is, that by which men govern; the first cause of the existence of the parties, of ambition, of tyranny, of privileges, of hatred! This is the monster in question! This is the Minotaur that drinks blood and devours by the billions! This is the fortress that's besieged, conquered, besieged again, reconquered, besieged yet again, to be once more reconquered by the parties!

Get rid of the administration, strangle the monster, knock down the Minotaur, demolish the fortress, and what will remain? Doctrines, nothing more! Individual doctrines now lacking any means of imposition! Isolated, timid and disconcerted doctrines that you will see running, out of breath, leaping, for protection and security, on the bosom of this great human doctrine: EQUITY!

Let's butcher this dragon, lined with claws, which the *National-ites* would tame for the benefit or Cavaignac, to have us bitten.

Which the socialists would tame for the benefit of Proudhon, to have us bitten.

Which the Orléanists would tame for the benefit of Mr. de Paris, to have us bitten.

Which the imperialists would tame for the benefit of Mr. Bonaparte, to have us bitten.

Which the legitimists would tame for the benefit of Mr. de Bourbon, to have us bitten.

Let's disperse the animal's claws around the municipalities; let's carefully guard them so they can't join together as one body again, and discord will vanish along with its only cause;

there will be nothing in France but free men who have, with respect for the rights of others, the same respect their own rights deserve, embracing one another in the fraternal ambition to work together for the common good. Mistrust thus loses the security of its hateful inspirations, capital encrusting itself in production, production relying on capital, and credit, national or individual, finds a footing!

XI.

Having reached this point of liberation, we are our own masters; nobody is higher than all the rest; nobody is beyond the common laws; national sovereignty becomes a reality, and universal suffrage takes on a democratic meaning.

Instead of having the inane and puerile right to choose our masters, which we have just been granted to do, we will choose delegates who, in turn, instead of being inspired by administrative rights, as is done at present, will be inspired by national rights, the precise definitions of which will follow the facts.

From this will emerge an administration that is simple, and, consequently, comprehensible; true, and consequently just. The program of accession by the French to all the posts will cease to be a crude lie, a wicked snare, the turpitude of which is demonstrated by the very powerlessness of specialized study to train men capable of figuring out the mechanism of a single section of the formidable administration that rules us.

And once our liberties have been saved, once the administration has been simplified, once the government has been stripped of its means of aggression, set a Frenchman at its head; let this Frenchman be named Cavaignac, Proudhon, d'Orléans, Bonaparte, Bourbon; I consider this far less important. Provided they are unable to usurp mastery over me, provided they can't forget their obligations to me, the men in office seem to deserve little serious attention; the names of those who serve me are of little importance. If they misbehave, I punish them; if they act well, they have only done their duty; I owe them nothing beyond their pay.

What I say of the name, I also mean of the title. If the head of a democratic administration is called president, king, emperor, satrap, sultan; let it be sir, citizen or majesty, it hardly matters! When the nation is truly sovereign, I'm sure of one thing, that the head of State, his name notwithstanding, can never be anything but the first servant of the nation, and that's enough; for, as soon as it's established, in fact, that a public official, salaried by the people, is nothing but the servant of the people, I know that the people will be insured against the official's passage, who, for his part, will have to disclose to the people that pays him, from which he makes his living, to which he owes his services, and which, consequently, is his master. When this is realized, there is no more indecisiveness in the city: the public's rights are defined, the nation is queen and the official is nothing but a hierarchical and remunerated member of a political domesticity which owes everything to all, and to which nobody personally owes anything.

If democracy is the destruction of the unworthy regime of bureaucracy;

If democracy is the consecration of the dignity of the citizen;

If democracy is the negation of ambition and its crimes, and at the same time the source of selflessness and its virtues;

If democracy is the government of the people, the government of oneself by oneself;

If democracy is only the pure and simple reign, and not the tyranny, of the administration;

It seems that I've got it this figured out.

XII.

Among peoples, there are only two points on which a divergence of opinions cannot exist. Two points where the common sense of all parties ends, without acceptation of nuances.

These two points are:

The repression of crime against persons and property, and defense of the territory.

Consult, on this point, all the sectarians of the various social schisms. Ask the socialists, the conservatives of this nameless regime of the *National*, the Orléanists, the imperialists, the legitimists; ask them, I say, whether murder and theft should be punished, whether the border should be protected; all will respond unanimously in the affirmative; for all, indistinctly, the person and what he has is sacred, the national territory is inviolable. These doctrines are the common, universal doctrines; before these the parties are effaced, they vanish; to these supreme points of the public rendezvous, all Frenchmen are in accord and fraternally shake hands.

Well then, why would we seek the genius of a government beyond this common reservoir of the aspirations of all? Why would we allow the introduction of a dose of individual affections to this potion prepared for the health of all?

Do you want a government that's strong by the assent of the public? A government whose existence is not threatened by the irritation and dexterity of the minority parties? Establish a serious governmental administration, which is a stranger to the bickering and miserable ambitions of individuals; a national administration, which embraces the parties by their rational and sensible basis, an administration whose power, limited, is restricted to supporting the execution of the decisions rendered in view of repressing crimes and offenses against people and property, and to regulate the relations and the differences that arise between the nation and the foreigner.

A government, whose attributions would be defined in this way, can't draw anyone's ire, without at the same instant being condemned by everyone; for, as it is only concerned precisely with those questions on which everyone agrees, it acts well or it acts badly, without contest. The sanction of its acts is in the conscience of all.

To keep a government sheltered from the revolutions, we must not allow it to meddle in the real lives of the citizens, it must not be allowed to touch the instincts, the tastes, the private interests of the citizens; for, these instincts, these tastes, these interests are varied and changing, while the rules of an administration are uniform and fixed.

A democratic government must remain forever as a social abstraction.

If I am commanded by a superior authority to think in one way and not another, to make exchanges on this condition and not that one, to be educated in this school or in this other book; to practice this profession rather than another, to love this instead of loving that, this is to tyrannize over me as much as if I were commanded to eat vegetables instead of meat; and a government with power over such extortionate details can't fail to irritate a people which is intelligent and in possession of any sense of human dignity.

If we dwell for a moment on the spirit of the institution that concerns me, it will be impossible for us to find a ministerial act that bears within it the violation of a liberty. A minister (I mean those whose administration is applied to the instincts, the tastes or interests), a minister cannot respect the public law, — not the written law — unless he doesn't do anything at all; for by taking action, he acts for all and in the place of all, it would be required, for him to act well and to harm nobody, for him to have an instinct for the present tendencies, a genius for the present tastes and an awareness of the present interests of everyone. That being so, one thing surprises me: that there are still men malicious enough or so profoundly incompetent as to not recoil from accepting a portfolio.

Who, then, would have suffered from the dispossession of the monarchical apparatus? A few civil servants!

Who would have benefited from it? All of France!

Who, then, suffers from the complete preservation of the monarchical apparatus? All of France!

Who benefits from this? A few civil servants!

I've said enough about this to show how, by taking the February revolution at its word, it was possible two attain both terms of the democratic equation: individual liberty and inexpensive government.

XIII.

But some people are far from accepting this argument. The theorists, our masters, find that ideas are preferable to facts. And this doctrine they maintain pays them a dividend that strongly encourages them to maintain it all the more.

In their view, as long as the tax keeps pouring in and as long as the rain respects, on the pediment of the public buildings, these words: Republic and Liberty, then we are republicans and we are free.

How strong such people are!

As strong as that clever character in the Arabic proverbs who, without touching the contents of the vase in any way, believed that by changing the label, he changed the liquid.

As strong as those burlesque geniuses in the farces at the fair, who think they're safe from fire on their clothes, because they're wearing a sign stating they have fire insurance.

Those people, I repeat, are extremely strong!

When we listen closely to the subtleties of their arguments, we'll hear much loud talk about the sovereignty of the people. Do you think it was ever permissible to insult the sovereign? You say: No! Well, it's after you're told that the people is sovereign that you have precisely the right to insult nothing but the people! As for me, I prefer to deny the sovereignty of the people and believe in the sovereignty of the government I'm told to respect.

I say that I prefer to believe in the sovereignty of the government; I'm even forced to believe this; everyone is quite forced to believe it like me; I don't exist, nobody here exists by themselves: our existence is far from our own. We only live civically, commercially, industrially, religiously, intellectually via the government!

Are we traveling without a letter of safe conduct, signed by it? Do we purchase a property, do we carry out a transaction in which it doesn't interpose itself? Do we profess a faith that it hasn't authorized? Do we seek education anywhere other than in the schools and in the books approved by its university? Do we publish anything other than what it allows us to publish? And, to press the analysis of this regulatory tyranny to the minutest details of triviality, do we smoke a cigar that it didn't sell us itself? Are we lawyers, doctors, professors, merchants, artists, mailmen, town criers, without our license from it? No! We don't exist, I tell you, we are all inert objects, parts belonging to a clever and complicated machine, the handle of which is in Paris!

Well, I say that that's an irregular situation, a situation as embarrassing for the government as it is disastrous for the nation.

I understand that it was possible for Richelieu to govern in this way, the France of the last centuries was completely, and by its own desires, under the king's crown. But woe to those who don't take into account differences in the times! Today, every citizen casts about and deliberates, and the control of the official certificates is everywhere!

XIV.

There is, however, in this sound part of the nation, in this nucleus of public common sense, people who are afraid to see clearly in this situation; people who can't resolve to understand without desperately having themselves bled out for the upkeep of five hundred thousand employees and as many as a thousand soldiers, they take a million men away from productive work and create, for the benefit of God knows what Minotaur, a parasitic officialdom whose formidable attitude withers all confidence and credit in the heart of the country, which is the only spring at which this same parasitism comes, however, to drink.

They perpetuate the crisis and they perpetuate it because they're afraid.

They're afraid of the socialists; they're afraid for their property; they're afraid for their religion; they're afraid for their family!

Are they afraid of the socialists?... Which socialists are they afraid of?

There are the socialists of Fourier.

There are the socialists of Pierre Leroux.

There are the socialists of Proudhon.

There are the socialists of Considérant.

There are the socialists of Louis Blanc.

There are the socialists of Cabet.

There are, *in fine*, the socialists that I know and then those that I don't and will never know, for socialism is split up, subdivided, diversified and separated into sects, like everything that's not defined, and socialism is certainly not defined.

Socialism is, in sum, a very obscure, very complicated, extraordinarily muddled philosophical system, which erudite men are obliged to study with minute attention, in order to, most often, end up comprehending none of it.

Socialism, according to what can be grasped from among all of its propositions, wants to make an immense hive of society, each cell of which will hold a citizen who will be commanded to remain silent and patiently wait for someone to give him alms from his own money. The great dispensers of these alms, the supreme preceptors of the common revenues, will form an état-major, passably funded, which, by raising his hand, will condescend to satisfy the public appetite; and who, if he happens to sleep longer than usual, will leave thirty-six million men without their breakfast.

Socialism is an attempt at geometric equilibrium, the demonstration of which, — based on a principle of immobility, — can never be based on human societies, which are essentially active and progressive.

Socialism is an abstract speculation, just as our present day administration is an abstract speculation: the people, which doesn't comprehend the latter, will do no better at understanding the former; and the people will never freely adopt what it doesn't understand.

Socialism, to sum up, wants to do the people's business, and it came too late for that, unless I'm quite mistaken.

But the socialists are the philosophers who have, to profess their doctrines, the same right as their opponents have to profess theirs. Just as it's the people's right to judge the former, it's also right for it to appreciate the latter.

Nobody can put themselves in the place of the people to pronounce the condemnation or to recognize the excellence of a doctrine; for, amid this diversity of tastes and inclinations that color our society, there is no doctrine that's wrong for everyone, nor is there one that's right for everyone.

Tolerance, in the theological order, has not resolved the problem of civil harmony; this problem also relates to tolerance in the social and political order.

The State religions have occasioned, across the centuries, discord and butchery, upon which we now look back with pity.

The State doctrines today cause a generous flowing of blood, from which our children will recoil to set up a monument to our shame!

We have destroyed the religions of the State; what are we waiting for to crush the doctrines of the State?

If we see no problem with those who want churches, temples or synagogues built, at their own expense, churches, temples and synagogues on their own land; I don't see what the problem would be if those who want convents, phalansteries or palaces built, at their own expense, convents, phalansteries and palaces on their own land.

And, if it's elementary to leave it to the Catholics, the Protestants and the Jews the faculty of maintaining, with their respective fees, priests, ministers and rabbis in these churches, temples, synagogues; it is no less elementary that the monks, the socialists and the courtiers have the right to maintain, with their respective fees, in these convents, phalansteries, palaces, the superiors, the patriarchs and the princes.

All these things are part of accommodating the tastes, the faith, the conscience of everyone, and one can be at the same time a monk, a socialist, a courtier and an excellent citizen; for the religions that should remain strangers to the laws of the State, aren't exempt from obedience to the laws of the State.

But what contains at least as much buffoonery as strangeness is the determination of a myriad of systems to attempt political campaigns; and their respective pretensions to make the whole nation help defray the cost of their establishment and the inauguration of their authority, whether public or national!

We only need to lend five hundred thousand bayonets to an acrobat, and the cabriole will become a social doctrine, while the will and whim of Pulcinella will become State law.

We are, certainly, quite close to that, and I won't deny that we're there already.

But I've digressed plenty. Let's return to our subject.

XV.

Do they fear for their property, for their religion, for their family?

The last sectarians of intolerance, those who mutter in our midst the words, still perceptible, alas, of humanity's tyrants, ceaselessly repeat their unruly periods on the subject of religion, property, the family.

These hilarious protectors of God and society aren't smart enough to realize that their asserted faculty of saving also necessarily implies the faculty of damning; they fail to realize, so seriously do they take their childish Quixotism, that the guard they set at the doors of the temple and the home, brings, as far as they're concerned, God and society under their discretion; they can't imagine, these adult children, that while saying to God and to society: "We have saved you from destruction"; is as if they told them that, "Without us, you would be no more; you owe us your life!"

Can you see from here an articulated apparatus of organic life, claiming a right of initiative on the existence of God and of society?

Can you see from here the moral and material universe depending on a degenerate quadrumane, who, at a snap of the fingers or due to a catarrh, could be made to pass from life to death?

Shame and pity!

Enough of this miserable and tumultuous jabbering!

Enough of this grandeur based on public humiliation!

Enough of this audacity based on fear!

Religion, property, family, which have passed through Genevan rationalism, Voltairean philosophism, the conventional confiscation, the dissolution of the social bonds of antiquity; religion, property, family are, in fact, invulnerable to attack by individuals; to defend them is to exploit them; to protect them is to despoil them!

Let the schemers of every stripe, along with those who think they're powerful enough to threaten them, let those who claim the ability to defend them; let all those, in short, who, living by intimidation and terrorism, have an interest in perpetuating universal panic, realize this fully: religion, property, the family, have never had any effective protector but time; they have never, consequently, been liable to attack from anything other than time.

Time, without anyone noticing, without anyone formulating a complaint, time changes everything: religion, property, family.

The present state of the church, with its degenerated discipline and its neutrality in the world's politics, would have made bold Hildebrand die of a fit of rage.

The present state of property, with its infinite subdivisions and the melancholy resignation of its chateaus, would make the great landholders of yesteryear turn in their graves.

The present state of the family, with the unremitting displacement of the individual, the allegiance to the domestic yoke, the disjunctions provoked by cosmopolitanism, would deeply wound the patriarchal traditions of our forebears.

The work of the future generation, if we could we see it, would be a shock to our prejudices, our habits, our way of being.

Thus, everything is modified without being destroyed, and the human mind can only accept what it's prepared for. Every day it opens to new interests, to which it becomes accustomed without any shock. After a period of time, the meeting of the new interests calls for a new institution which, if it came all at once previously, would have surprised and offended everyone, but which, coming from the providential order of succession, has offended nobody and has satisfied everyone.

Let it be said without any fear.

Fear is only self-condemnation, and when one is condemned, executioners are never lacking!

XVI.

The hypothesis of dispossession has been presented.

Nobody can believe in the corruptibility of majorities, without at the same moment denying human reason and the principle of its demonstration. If majorities are incorruptible, they are fair: and the elementary law of fairness is the respect for vested rights.

Vested rights have been respected even among peoples where the means of acquisition were denied to majorities. How could this right be violated with us, where acquisition, still very shackled, can still be considered public.

Say nothing to be about brigandry, when it's proved that it can only be what minorities do, and when its exercise requires its organization.

Say nothing to be about brigandry, when instead of a plan of uncombinable organization, all anyone can show me is a few cries in the street or some argument from a club.

The whole people is not responsible for the exceptional insanity of a few minds. Madmen are humanity's lost children!

Brigandry cannot be organized. I'm mistaken, it can be organized, here's how: Place, in each commune, an authority that's more jealous of its exclusive rights than the public law; establish hateful, intolerant, and fanatical magistrates in each *arrondissement*, in each *département*: at the top of this hierarchy, set a supreme chief who is blinded by the pride of domination, and nursed on impious dogmas; give this man four or five hundred thousand armed men to support him, and dispossession as the watchword, and the violation of vested rights will be achieved.

But I'm told that the above scene is nothing other than the administrative organization, founded by the constitutions. I allow as much, and it follows from this that a miscreant who doesn't seize the administration of the State will be nobody to fear. But this also means that this administration suppresses us so much that we are completely vulnerable to the first audacious man whom chance brings our way.

Give the people dispossession as their watchword, and this watchword will be bogged down with the integrity of the majority.

Let this watchword come from the administration whose systematic webs embrace every individual and the whole territory, and the supreme thought is propagated like electricity, vanishing into the blood!

This is the only possible way to organize brigandry, and this, definitively, is how the government of the representative monarchies might be put to use.

Are those who possess afraid of being dispossessed in isolation by those who have nothing? I mourn for them while condemning them, for by this they show me how they would behave if they had nothing.

And yet, they are mistaken; they are more upright than they think; they argue from the perspective of the needs that their wealth has given them. I can see that if they were suddenly deprived of the satisfaction of these needs, which have, in a way, become natural for them, they would have to suffer, and they argue under the sway of this impression; but what they forget is that, if they didn't have their wealth, they also wouldn't have their needs.

Besides, can someone who comes to dispossess me today not, in virtue of the same principle, be dispossessed tomorrow? And if time passed like this, mutually dispossessing each other, what would happen to production?

Can such an absurd state of affairs be feared by sensible people, the day after a revolution when everything was at the discretion of the masses, and when perversity, in an exceptional state, was drowned in public integrity?

If the majority, which owns nothing, had an instinct for dispossession, the possessing minority would long since have known what line to hold.

If there are miscreants in our localities, let's take note of them; this is easy to do; and if we find few or none of them, let's not think that we have a monopoly on fairness; people are the same everywhere.

That the dominating and insolent rage of certain men dismembers, by the magnanimity of the masses, and discounts the human character, this is conceivable: the dogma of impropriety is the reason of tyrannies, and the security of tyrants is based on the hatred and mistrust of citizens for each other. As for me, separate from the parties to remain a man, I defend humanity because of *esprit de corps.*

XVII.

But this is what I mean:

If socialism attained the government, it might impose itself. I expected this objection.

It is therefore true that, as philosophers, as apostles of a doctrine, as professors, the socialists offer no cause for concern. All opinions can therefore be expressed without danger, provided that these opinions don't aspire to the government.

But what! We feel that the public's common sense will overcome the absurdity, but we're afraid of being governed by the absurd? So, we acknowledge that we can be governed despite common sense? So, we acknowledge that our religion can be assaulted the moment anyone starts to govern us? But, if we admit this, we are in constant danger of being handed over! But I shouldn't say "in danger"; we have already been handed over, for, in matters of public security, probabilities are certainties.

At the very moment when we acknowledge that someone might do us violence they do us violence; this law is inexorable, necessary, and inherent in any state of dependency.

It isn't, therefore, the socialists we should worry about, or try to get rid of; we should fear, we should banish the institution in virtue of which they can strike us. This institution alone is bad, is dangerous, and, no matter who is placed at the head of this institution, they will immediately be as dangerous as the socialists; Firstly, because he can become so, secondly, because he can be surprised and defeated by the socialists, and, finally, because his system can be as bad as or worse than theirs.

As long as unlimited liberty of opinion doesn't exist in France, a doctrine will be forced, to be visible, to try to overthrow the government; for its only means of action will be to become a State doctrine, to govern; and, as long as a doctrine of State governs, it will necessarily consider all other doctrines as dangerous rivals, and will outlaw them.

This is how we will continue to see these impious struggles to which society brings its children and its money; these combats of scheming and ambition, which I would call absurd if they weren't atrocious, and whose outcome, attacked today only to be celebrated tomorrow, makes crime or heroism a simple matter of the date.

XVIII.

It is, therefore, established that socialism is not more fearful in itself than any other philosophical doctrine. It is assumed that it can only become dangerous on condition of governing. Which means that nobody is dangerous who doesn't govern; from which it follows that whoever governs already is or can become dangerous; from which also comes the strict conclusion that the nation can have no other public enemy than the government.

With this in mind, it is beyond doubt that the only important thing in modern times, the only one which our representatives have not concerned themselves with, consists in simplifying the administrative organism to the degree demanded by individual liberty, which has been without any guarantee to day, and by the reduction of taxation, which will be impossible to achieve as long as we persist in the path cut by the big-budget governments.

The present governmental institution is the same as that of the last year, and that of the last year summed up all the powers of Louis XIV, with the only difference the unity of action of the royal tutelage is found to be shared among six or seven ministerial departments, set in play by a parliamentary majority. Can we be a free people, as long as our existence is regulated from the civic to the hygienic realms?

If we set up the guarantee of our individual liberty, if we resolve to move of our own accord, the nation will regain this force which was seized or usurped from it; this necessary force, indispensable to balancing the popular prerogatives with governmental attributions.

If the nation regained all its force, the assembly which came from its heart, wouldn't so quickly forget where the real master is, where the true and sovereign has his camp, and, in the contract which would have passed between France and its stewards, the latter would have no means to become the master of the former.

XIX.

Along with governmental mastery, as once possessed by the fallen administrations, and as we have possessed it so far, we might boldly distrust any man who has seriously accepted public office; what is required is the reduction in the staff of both of those formidable armies that impose at the same time on the liberties and the wealth of France: the army of the bureaucrats and that of the barracks. He can be distrusted, consequently, to proclaim liberty, this occurs and it makes me laugh, but he can be defied to make this liberty a reality and make it anything but a dead letter!

With all the more reason can he be defied to lower taxes. Not only this, he is forbidden to keep them at sixteen hundred million, a monstrous figure, whose insufficiency, however, can easily be demonstrated by anyone who isn't the minister of finance.

This, in the real world, is what the governmental mastery accomplishes: slavery and ruin.

This mastery, by assuming the right to regulate as it likes the movements and thoughts of each citizen, has produced, in the moral order, a result which is really no less deplorable! It has legalized everything.

Well, one would go strangely wrong to believe that legality bears in its quibbling entrails the seeds of human integrity!

Legislation in France is not based on respect for individuals; it is based on the principle of the violation of public law; for, at its base is consecrated, *lèse-majesté*, respect for the king, the emperor, the government. The law has never had any social sanction among us; it has had only royal sanction, the sanction of the governmental supremacies, the characteristic of which has always been to protect the smaller number.

Our legislation is therefore immoral, for it is unpopular!

This legislation is, besides, necessarily subsequent to the vices that it wishes to repress, it is really only the consecration of these vices. A code teaches me far more about what I should avoid than what I should do; and, in my mind, I do quite suitably well when I abstain from doing what is wrong. And a fundamental snare can be introduced into the mind of the public; for the skilled man, confronted with the law, finds he looks just the same as a truly virtuous man.

The legally conformant man is he against whom no grievance has been proved; but a clever man is not unentitled to claim the benefits of the same definition! He who does evil in the dark, without witnesses and around the habitually avoided pitfall of the prohibitive letter of the laws, even he who enjoys the protection of the judge, is also a man against whom no grievance has been proved. He, too, is an upright man! And he would be all the more mistaken to follow the law of social equity, the rule of morality, as the legal Gospel is present before his eyes, as he has free rein as to unexpected situations, as he provides, by his knowhow, for the expected situations, and for whom the judge's friendship remains intact.

According to legality, therefore, fairness emanates from the tribunal's judgment, and the public's conscience is bested by the conscience of the law-code.

Legality! But by pressing the social body towards pure and simple legality, the governments have created and produced fraud, that poetry of the fighting ring!

Man, called upon to be clever enough to avoid the snares set for him by the lawgiver, no longer makes the effort of hypocrisy. After having skillfully escaped the foresight of the law, he boasts about it, as if his contemporaries should respect him for it; he outplayed the code, and his victory is assured: he's a superior being!

It goes without saying that our legislation, producing scholarly volumes, the examination and interpretation of which is only for the erudite, has been unable to attain to the morality of the simple folk who always have been and who haven't ceased to constitute the daily bread of the jurists.

Here, then, is what has been left for us by the work, so highly praised, of the legislative assemblies: a famous code, the tombstone raised by the public mourning on the grave of virtue! Each vice, in passing, has come to trace out its own motto on this frozen book, and, the more numerous these mottos are, the finer the code is, and the finer the code is, the more perverted society is.

XX.

One thing we should never tire of repeating is that there is only morality among free peoples, and free peoples are those whose government, speaking the national language very little, mostly speaks foreign languages; the government of democracies is mainly diplomatic.

Among us, government means the Republic, the State, Society. These words, in effect, like red Republic, tricolor Republic, etc., which try our patience, mean nothing but red government, tricolor government, etc. For the official world, therefore, the government is the Republic.

Who do we think is mistaken here?

People today, far different from those of yesterday, can feel, if they don't understand, that their being and their having are completely separate from the administration. They feel it so strongly that, even if they allow, by a leftover habit, a government to be established on the old model, they effectively withdraw from it, they don't put their confidence in it, and will only give it material support while grumbling, or due to compulsion or fear; they feel this so well that they have decided to control, in the public square, the doings of the administration. And, a power, whose acts are all controlled, is struck by decline under the law, for it is challenged.

But this error, which consists in shielding all of society with the governmental symbol, is powerfully embedded in the public beliefs.

The power of tradition has made this a national article of faith, which daily finds itself in more and more direct opposition to the will and feeling of the public.

Thus, everyone knows that a popular movement endangers nothing but the official fortunes of a few men; but the public papers and the proclamations, stating that the movement is a threat to society, the nation admits it without explaining itself.

If I wanted to adopt the way capable men reason, using in their own interest the forces confided to them by society, this would lead me to an odd conclusion, a deceptive commentary on the tumultuous spectacle of the revolutions!

XXI.

I've seen, in the few years that my memory can grasp, a very respectable number of popular movements.

When these movements failed at the first paving stone, their authors were seized bodily, cast into the dungeons, judged and condemned as criminals against the State. The proclamations affixed to all the walls of Paris and dispatched to the least town in the départements, taught society that it had just been saved.

Surely, at this news, I should logically think that if, by some misunderstanding, authority had overstepped its bounds, if armed force had weakened, if the movement had exceeded its limits, this was carried out by society: France was pillaged, sacked, set on fire, lost!

But when these movements, overcoming all obstacles, overthrowing authority, with armed force, have held their course and reached their goal, their authors have been let to victory, saluted as heroes and elevated to the highest offices. Proclamations attached on all the walls of Paris and dispatched even to the least town of the départements, informed society that it had just been saved.

Thus society, constantly endangered, is always saved!

Who saves it? Those who endanger it.

Who endangers it? Those who save it.

Which means that society is never more completely lost than when it is saved.

And that it's never better saved than when it is lost.

When I said that by adopting the arguments of the skilled men who use, in their personal interest, the forces that society confides in them, that would lead me to an odd conclusion!

Odd, indeed, and logically explicable by the facts.

Thus, with 23 February in mind, it remains established that, according to the *Journal des Débats*, the *Constitutionnel*, the *Siècle* and all the papers that defended the social order, that the agitators in Paris, on this date, were only unacknowledged troublemakers seeking nothing less than the subversion, overthrow and ruin of society.

These unacknowledged troublemakers were victorious the day after and suddenly, each citizen said what they liked, wrote, published what they liked, did what they liked, went where they liked, left, entered when they liked; enjoyed, in brief, their primordial liberties to the whole extent of the social art, in the most complete security, in favor of the most fraternal urbanity. Society, in short, was saved in each of its members.

And this happened on the very day when, according to the friends of order, society was lost.

Thus, again, in the words of the same defenders of the social order, to whom, for reasons known to it alone, this time the *National* came and added that: "the agitators of June were only unacknowledged troublemakers, who sought nothing less than the subversion, the overthrow and the ruin of society.

These troublemakers failed and, at once, each citizen was quartered at home, visited minutely in their houses, disarmed, cast into dungeons for the mere denunciation of malevolence, reduced to the most absolute silence, placed under the mutinous surveillance of a police state of siege and ruled by the cutting, pointed and unthinking law of the saber. Society was therefore lost in each of its members.

And this happened the very day when, according to the friends of order, this time including the *National*, society had been saved.

From which I am forced to conclude, as I've already said and shown, that society is never more completely lost than when it's saved and that it's never more saved than when it's lost.

This spectacle, O Frenchmen, as delicate as it is subtle, is being played out before nations and before posterity, in the most intelligent country in the universe!

How indecent it is!

XXII.

All I'm doing here is pointing out the facts; I take and indicate things as they appear to me. As for commentary, I'll limit myself to repeating what I've said elsewhere: I don't believe in the efficacy of armed revolutions, and for a very simple reason, which is that I don't believe in the efficacy of armed governments.

An armed government is a brutal thing, for it has no rule but force.

An armed revolution is also a brutal thing, for it has no rule but force.

But when one is ruled by the arbitrariness of barbarity, we must surely rebel like barbarians; and, faced with the weapons that are crossed over their chests, the parties must certainly arm themselves too.

As long as a government, instead of improving conditions, only improves the condition of a few people, a revolution, the inevitable end of this government, will be only a substitution of people instead of being a conversion of things.

Armed governments are sectarian authorities, party administrations.

Armed revolutions are sectarian wars, party campaigns.

The nation is as alien to armed government as it is to armed revolution; but if a revolutionary party happens to be more immediately concerned than the nation by the governmental party, it also happens that, on a given day, the concerned nation in turn murmurs against the government, and this precise instant is when it gains the moral support of the people, when the revolutionary party begins to fight.

Hence the sort of public consecration given to the bloody juggling which, on the pompous pretext of revolutions, conceal the impertinence of a few valets in a rush to become the masters.

When the people has fully understood the position reserved for it in these saturnalia that it pays for, when it sees what an ignoble and stupid role it has been made to play, it will know that armed revolution is a heresy from the point of view of principles; it will know that violence is the antipodes of the law; and, once based on morality and the tendencies of the violent parties, whether governmental or revolutionary, it will make its revolution by itself, by the sole force of the law: the force of inertia, the refusal to participate. In the refusal of assistance are found the abrogation of the laws on legal murder and the proclamation of equity.

This supreme act of national sovereignty which I see coming from here, not as the result of a calculation, but as the expression of a necessary law, as an inevitable product of administrative greed, of the extinction of credit and the dire advent of immiseration. This revolution, which will be French and not only Parisian, will tear France away from Paris and lead it back to the municipality; then, and only then, will the national sovereignty be a fact, for it will be based on the sovereignty of the commune.

To these words *sovereignty of the commune,* all these great geniuses who have dragged patriotism before the bar of vocabulary to make the Republic a question of words, raise an objection in the thrice-holy name of unity.

Unity! It's the right moment to discuss it. Amid the divisions tearing the country apart, I would ask what the lame showoffs, who speak in the name of the national unity, have done with it!

Unity! I know only one way to destroy it; which is to try to effectuate it by force. If someone had the power to act on the planets and if, to effectuate the unity of the solar system, he tried to force them to stick together at the center, he would break their balance and bring back chaos!

There is someone here who is more unitary than the "unitaries"; this someone is the French people; and if France doesn't understand that it must soon exit the stomach of the administration, lest it be dissolved there, this won't be my fault, or that of the coarse peritonea who perform the digestion.

XXIII.

Let's say it, though; the result of an armed revolution, assuming that this revolution is generously interpreted by a big-hearted man, all-powerful as to opinion, upright, selfless and a democrat like Washington, — the result of an armed revolution, I've said, might be turned to the benefit of the public law.

With the tyrants overthrown, before any others take their place, there always appears, on the ruins of tyranny, one man who is greater than the rest, a man whom everyone sees, whom everyone listens to, and he is the master of the debris; he can scatter it or reconstruct it as he pleases.

If Lamartine had had a mind for the facts, as he had a mind for things of intelligence, then 24 February would have been the birthday of the French Republic, instead of being only invective.

France, on this date, was expecting everything from this radiant man whom the national sympathies had spontaneously made the powerful maneuver of the destinies of the people.

All he had to tell us, in the harmonious rhythm of his refined language, was:

"The government of kings is abolished: France is no longer at the Hôtel-de-Ville!

"Your masters have vanished; they will not be replaced!

"Their law was in force; force has disappeared: it will not return!

"You have returned to yourselves; the foreigner will hear from me that you are free.

"Look out for yourselves; I'll keep my eye on the border!"

Certainly, after such substantial declarations, our Representatives, whoever they were, wouldn't have lost sight of the fact that they had to define the national law, and not the fanatical law of the governments.

Perhaps, Lamartine would have fallen victim to ambitious men left without prey. The despair of the tyrant apprentices would have been unleashed upon him; but his death, like that of the great citizens, would have been productive! And since, as he puts it, *ideas are nourished by human blood*, his own would have remained on the cusp of the free era, as an eternal protest against the tyranny of the liveries!

Unfortunately, instead of disseminating the elements of despotism, he gathered them instead to reconstruct it; the edifice is now complete, including the keystone. He isn't the one residing in it, but it is inhabited; no worse, perhaps, but no better.

Well! the moment has come to leave words behind and get to the action!

The moment has come to know what democracy means!

The moment has come for all Frenchmen, in every artery where a drop of Gaulish blood still flows who, from Diocletian to Charlemagne, protested against the tyranny of the empire, to rise again like free citizens, and cry out against the cowardice and incompetence of the men of the people, of the Republican individualities, about our ruined credit, our terrified capital, our paralyzed industries, our suspended works, our extinct commerce, our idle products; our France, finally, so ungrateful, so alienated, so venal, so prostituted, so debased, so inhospitable, so alien to ourselves, so polluted by the taxman, and so close to the contempt of their children, that they soon won't have enough love in their hearts to courageously resist the attacks of their abductors!

This moment has come, for we are in the presence of a decisive spectacle; on one hand, it's the government that distrusts the nation.

On the other hand, it's the nation that distrusts the government.

And it is absolutely necessary for the government to devour the country, or for the country to absorb the government.

THE END.

MANIFESTO

L'Anarchie, Journal de l'Ordre

No. 1, April 1850

ANARCHY IS ORDER

If I were concerned about the sense commonly attached to certain words, a vulgar error having made *anarchy* synonymous with *civil war*, I'd be horrified by the title that I've placed at the head of this publication, since I'm horrified by civil war.

At the same time, I honor and congratulate myself for never having been part of a group of conspirators or a revolutionary battalion; for this I honor and congratulate myself because it establishes, on one hand, that I've been upright enough never to trick the people, and, on the other, that I've been capable enough to avoid being tricked by ambitious men. I've seen many, I won't say without any emotion, but at least with the utmost calm, many fanatics and charlatans come and go, pitying the former and feeling supreme contempt for the latter. And when, having trained my enthusiasm to pounce only within the strict limits of syllogism, I've sought, after the blood-red struggles, to tally up the welfare contributed by each cadaver, and the total came to zero; and zero means nothing.

I abhor nothing; therefore, I abhor civil war.

So, if I've written ANARCHY on the frontispiece of this journal, it isn't, therefore, to leave this word with the common, but mistaken meaning given to it, as I'll explain shortly, by the governmentalist sects, but rather to restore it to the etymological rights that the democracies concede it.

Anarchy is the negation of governments. The governments, whose wards we are, quite naturally found nothing better to do than to raise us in fear and horror of the principle of their destruction. But since, in turn, the governments are the negation of individuals or the people, it is rational that the people, having become clear-sighted as to the essential truths, would associate its own negation with all the horror it had initially felt for the negation of its masters.

Anarchy is an old word, but for us this word expresses a modern idea, or rather a modern interest, for ideas are the daughters of interests. History has called the state of a people in whose heart are many competing governments *anarchic* but the case is quite different for a people who, wishing to be governed, lacks a government precisely because it has too much of it, and also different is the state of a people who, wishing to govern itself, lacks a government precisely because it refuses it. The anarchy of

[margin note top: for ones... the idea of pure democracy specifically]

[margin note left: Anarchism is something specific to our historic moment and could not emerge earlier]

antiquity was indeed civil war, and not because it expressed the absence, but instead the plurality of governments, competition, the struggle of the gubernative races.

The modern notion of the absolute social truth, or of pure democracy, has opened a whole series of fields of knowledge or interests that radically change the terms of the traditional equation. Thus, anarchy, which, from the relative or monarchic point of view, signifies civil war, is nothing less, as an absolute or democratic thesis, than the true expression of social order.

In effect:

[margin note: This line is doing the work of connecting above and below. It says liberty = equality]

Anarchy means the negation of the government;
The negation of the government means the affirmation of the people;
The affirmation of the people means individual liberty;
Individual liberty means the sovereignty of each;
The sovereignty of each means equality;
Equality means solidarity or fraternity;
Fraternity means social order;
Therefore, anarchy means social order.

On the other hand:

Government means the negation of the people;
The negation of the people means the affirmation of political authority;
The affirmation of political authority means individual dependence;
Individual dependence means caste supremacy;

[margin note bottom: Liberty = Equality; Government = Caste]

Caste supremacy means inequality;
Inequality means antagonism;
Antagonism means civil war;
Therefore, government means civil war.

I don't know if what I've just said is novel, or eccentric, or frightening. I don't know this and I don't care.

What I do know is that I can boldly bring my arguments into play against all the prose of white and red governmentalism past, present and future. The truth is that, in this terrain, which is that of a free man, a stranger to ambition, diligent in labor, contemptuous of command, rebellious against submission, I defy all the arguments of bureaucratism, all the paid-up logicians and all the hacks of the tax, whether monarchic or republican, call it progressive, proportional, land, capitalist, annuitant, or consumer.

Yes, anarchy is order; for government is civil war.

When my intelligence sees through the miserable details on which the daily polemic is based, I find that the internal wars which have always decimated humanity are connected to this one cause, i.e., overthrowing or preserving the government.

As a political thesis, to butcher each other has always meant to devote oneself to the keeping or the bringing about of a government. Show me a place where people commit murder *en masse* and out in the open, and I'll show you a government at the head of the carnage. If you try to explain civil war otherwise than as one government trying to come and a government refusing to leave, you're wasting your time: you won't find anything.

The reason is simple.

A government is founded.

At the very instant when the government is founded it has its creatures, and, subsequently, its supporters; and at the very moment it gains its supporters, it also finds its opponents. And the germ of civil war is fertilized by this single fact, for you can't make the government, invested with omnipotence, treat its opponents like its supporters. You can't expect the favors it bestows to be distributed equally between its friends and its enemies. You can't keep the former from being pampered and the latter persecuted. You can't, therefore, keep this inequality from producing, sooner or later, a conflict between the party of privilege and the party of the oppressed. In other terms, given a government, you can't avoid the favor that establishes privilege, which provokes division, which creates antagonism, which prepares a civil war.

Therefore, government is civil war.

Now it's enough to be, on one side, the supporter, and on the other, the opponent of the government, to determine the outcome of a conflict between citizens; if it's shown that outside of the love or hatred one feels for the government, the civil war has no reason to exist, that means that it's enough, to establish the peace, if the citizens renounce, on one hand, to be the supporters, and on the other, to be the opponents of the government.

And, to cease to attack or to defend the government in order to make civil war impossible, is nothing less than to forget about it, to cast it aside, to suppress it in order to lay the foundations for social order.

And, if to suppress the government is, on one hand, to establish order, it is, on the other hand, to lay the foundations for anarchy; therefore, order and anarchy are parallel to each other.

Therefore, anarchy is order.

Before passing to the further developments of this subject, I beg the reader to watch out for the bad impression that he might get from the personal form that I've adopted to facilitate the argument and speed the flow of ideas. In this presentation, ME means far less the writer than the reader or the hearer; ME is humanity.

THAT THE TRADITIONAL COLLECTIVE REASON IS A FICTION

Put in these terms, the question turns out to have, above socialism and the inextricable chaos that the heads of that school have made of it, the merit of clarity and precision. I am an anarchist, i.e., a man of free inquiry, a political and social Huguenot, I deny everything, I affirm only myself; for the one truth that is materially and morally demonstrated to me, with tangible, perceptible, and intelligible proofs, the only truth that is true, striking, non-arbitrary and not subject to interpretation, is me. Behold me now, as a positive fact; all else is abstract and relates to mathematics, unknowns: I don't have to worry about it.

Society's entire *raison d'être* is in a vast combination of material and *private* interests; the collective interest, or the State, in consideration of which dogma, philosophy and politics together have, to date, called for the full or partial abnegation of individuals and their property, is a pure fiction, the theocratic invention of which has served as a foundation for the good fortune of all clergies, from Aaron to Bonaparte. This interest only exists to the extent that it's legislatively apprehensible.

It never has been true, it never will be true, it cannot be true that there is any interest on Earth that's superior to mine, an interest to which I owe the sacrifice, even partial, of my interests, there is nothing on Earth but men, I am a man, my interest is equal to anyone else's; I cannot owe anything but what is owed to me; I can only owe what is my due; nobody can return me anything but what I've given them, but I owe nothing to he who gives me nothing; therefore, I owe nothing to the collective reason, even if it be the government, for the government gives me nothing, and even less can it give me anything but what it has taken from me. In any case, the best judge I know of the opportunity of the advances I should make and of the probability of their returning, is me; in this respect there is no advice, no lesson, nor above all, any order that I need to receive from anyone.

This argument: it's not only the right, but also the duty of everyone to apply it to themselves or hold to it. This is the true, intuitive, incontestable and indestructible foundation of the only human interest that deserves attention: private interest, individual prerogative.

Does this mean that I mean to utterly deny the collective interest? No, to be sure. But, since I hate to speak in vain, I won't discuss it. After having laid the foundations of private interest, I act with regard to the collective interest as I should act *vis-à-vis* society when I've introduced the individual into it. Society is the inevitable and necessary consequence of the aggregation of individuals; the collective interest, for the same reason, is a providential and fatal deduction from the aggregation of all the private interests. The collective interest can only be complete if private interests remain intact, for, since the collective interest can only mean the interests of everyone, it's enough if, in society, the interests of a single individual are wronged for the collective interest to no longer represent the interests of all and, consequently to cease to exist.

It is true that the collective interest is a natural deduction from private interests in the necessary order of things, that the community won't take my field to make a road, or won't require the conservation of my forest to keep the air pure without indemnifying me as broadly as possible. It's my interest that governs here, individual rights outweigh collective rights; I have the same interest as the community to have a road and breathe healthy air, yet, I would chop down my forest and keep my field to myself if the community failed to indemnify me, but just as it has an interest in indemnifying me, my interest is in yielding, of such stuff is the collective interest, which springs from the nature of things. There is another one, which is accidental and abnormal: war; this is outside the law, it makes the law and always does it well; we only need to worry about the one that's permanent.

But when you call "the collective interest" the one in virtue of which you close my establishment, forbid me to practice in a certain industry, confiscate my journal or my book, violate my liberty, keep me from being a lawyer or a doctor by virtue of my private studies and my clientele, intimate to me an order not to sell this, not to buy that; when, finally, you call the collective interest that thing you invoke to keep me from making my living out in the open, in the way that best pleases me and under the control of everyone, I declare that I don't understand you, or, rather, that I understand you too well.

To safeguard the collective interest, a man who heals his fellow unlawfully is condemned; — it's an evil to do good *illegally*; — on the pretext that he hasn't received a certificate, is to keep a man from defending the cause of a citizen (sovereign) who has put his trust in it; a writer is arrested; a publisher is put out of business; a peddler is imprisoned; a man who shouted, or who wears a certain hat, is dragged into court.

What do I get from all this misfortune?

What do you get from it?

I run from the Pyrenees to la Manche and from the Ocean to the Alps, and I ask each of the thirty-six million Frenchmen what they get from these stupid cruelties wrought in their name upon poor wretches whose families now groan, worried about their creditors, whose businesses perish and who might kill themselves in despair or turn into criminals from rage once they escape their current tribulations. And, on this question, nobody knows what mean, everyone refuses any responsibility for what's happening; the misery of the victims hasn't benefited anyone; tears have been shed, interests have been harmed to the point of complete loss. And this savage monstrosity is what you call the collective interest. I, for my part, affirm that if this collective interest wasn't a shameful error, I would call it the vilest sort of plunder.

But let's set aside this furious and blood-red fiction, and say that the only way to perfect the collective interest is safeguard private interests, it has been proven, abundantly proven, that the most important thing, in matters of sociability and economy, is to release, before all else, the private interests.

I'm therefore right when I say that the only social truth is the natural truth, the individual, myself.

THAT THE INDIVIDUALISTIC DOGMA IS THE ONLY FRATERNAL DOGMA

Don't talk to me about revelation, tradition, the Chinese, Phoenician, Egyptian, Hebrew, Greek, Roman, German, or French philosophies; outside of my faith or my religion, for which I'm accountable to nobody, I've no need to ramble about my ancestors; I have no ancestors! For me, the creation of the world dates from my birth; for me, the end of the world must occur the day I hand back to the elementary mass, the apparatus and the breath which constitute my individuality. I am the first man, I will be the last. My history is the complete summation of the history of humanity; I don't know, I don't want to know any other. When I suffer, what benefit do I derive from the enjoyments of other people? When I enjoy something, how do those who suffer get any benefit from my pleasures? What do I care what happened before me? How am I affected by what will happen after I'm gone? I must neither serve as a sacrifice in honor of extinct generations, nor as an example to posterity. I shut myself up within the circle of my own existence, and the only problem I need to solve is that of my own welfare. I have only one doctrine, this doctrine has only one formula, this formula contains one word only: ENJOYMENT!

He who confesses this is right; he who denies it is an impostor.

That this is crude individualism, native selfishness, I don't disagree, I confess it, I'm aware of it, I boast of it! Show me, so I can interrogate him, anyone who would pity and fault me for it. Does my selfishness (*égoïsme*) harm you in some way? If you say no, then you have no objection to raise, for I'm free in everything that can't harm you. If you say yes, you're a crook, for my selfishness, which is only the simple appropriation of me to myself, an appeal to my identity, an affirmation of my individual, a protest against all supremacy; if you recognize yourself as suffering offense by my act of self-possession, by my retaining of my own person, i.e., of the least contestable of my properties, then you're saying that I belong to you, or at least that you have ambitions about me; you're a proprietor of men, established or in process of establishment, a monopolist, a covetor of another's goods, a crook.

There is no middle ground: selfishness is a right, or it's theft; I either belong to myself, or I must be someone's possession. You can't say that I renounce myself for the benefit of all, since all must likewise renounce themselves, in this idiotic game nobody would win anything but what they'd already lost, and would consequently be even, i.e., without benefit, which would obviously make this renunciation absurd. If, then, the abnegation of all fails to benefit all, it must necessarily benefit some; these some are, then, the owners of all the rest, and these are most likely the ones complaining of my selfishness.

Well! Let them encase the values I've just subscribed to, in their honor.

Every man is selfish; whoever ceases to be one is a thing. He who claims not to be one is a crook.

Oh yes, I understand: the word sounds bad; up to present you have used it against those who were discontent with their own goods, to those who attracted to themselves the goods of others; but people like these are within the human order, you're the one who isn't. By complaining of their rapacity, do you know what you're doing? You're showing your imbecility. You've thought, up to now, that there were tyrants! Well, you were mistaken, there are only slaves: where nobody obeys, nobody commands either.

Listen to this: the dogma of resignation, of abnegation, of self-renunciation has been preached to the populations.

What has been the result?

The papacy and the royalty, by God's grace, from which the episcopal and monkish, princely and noble castes come.

Oh! The people is resigned, is annihilated, has long since renounced itself.

Was this a good thing?

What do you think?

Sure, the greatest gift you could ever give the bishops who are somewhat disconcerted, the assemblies which have replaced the king, the ministers who have replaced the princes, the prefects who have replaced the dukes, the great vassals, the sub-prefects who have replaced the barons, the petty vassals, and the entire series of subaltern officers who we have instead of the feudal knights, vidames and lordlings; the greatest gift, I said, that you could ever give this entire budgetary nobility, is to return as quickly as possible into the traditional dogma of the resignation, abnegation and renunciation of yourselves. You will also find there not a few protectors who will advise you to despise riches at the risk of ridding you of them; you will find not a few fanatics who, to save your soul, will preach continence, except in cases of saving your women, daughters or sisters embarrassment. We have no lack, thank God, of devoted friends who would be damned for our sake. If we resolved to win Heaven by following the old path of blessedness, from which they politely depart in order, no doubt, to open the way for us.

Why don't all these continuers of the ancient hypocrisy seem any better balanced on the trestles constructed by their forerunners?

Why indeed?

Because abnegation is on its way out and individualism is on the rise; because man finds himself beautiful enough to toss the mask and finally show himself as he is.

Abnegation is slavery, debasement, abjectness; it's the king, it's the government, it's tyranny, it's struggle, it's civil war.

Individualism, on the contrary, is liberation, greatness, nobility; it's man, it's the people, it's liberty, it's fraternity, it's order.

THAT THE SOCIAL CONTRACT IS A MONSTROSITY

Let everyone in society affirm themselves personally, and only themselves, and individual sovereignty will find a foundation, then there will be no more room for the government, all supremacy will be destroyed, man will be man's equal.

If that happened, what would remain? What would remain is what all governments have vainly tried to destroy; what would remain is the essential and imperishable basis of nationality; what would remain is the town (*la commune*), which all the powers disrupt and disorganize in an effort to appropriate it; what remains is the municipality (*la municipalité*), the fundamental organization, that primordial existence which resists all disorganization and all destruction. The town has its own administration, its own jury, its own judicatures; it would improvise these if it lacked them.

France, were it organized municipally by itself, would be democratically self-organized. There is nothing to do, as to the inner organism, all is ready-made; the individual is free and sovereign in the town; the municipality, as the complex individual, is free and sovereign in the nation.

Now, should the nation, or the town, have a synthetic and central organ to regulate certain common, *material and determinate* interests, and to serve the interlocutor between the community and the foreigner? That isn't a question for anyone; and I don't see any cause for concern about things that everyone considers rational and necessary. What is in question is the government; but an arbitration and a chancellery, due to the initiative of the towns, which have retained their self-mastery, can constitute, if they wish, an administrative commission, but not a government.

Do you know what makes a mayor aggressive in the commune? It's the prefect. Get rid of the prefect, and the mayor can only rely on the individuals who appointed him; the liberty of all is secured.

An institution which depends on the municipality isn't a government; a government is an institution which the municipality obeys. We can't call that on which individual influence has an impact a government; government is what we call that which crushes individuals under the weight of its influence.

What is in question, in a word, is not *civic action*, the nature and character of which I will soon explain, it's the *social contract*.

There is not, there cannot be a social contract, firstly because society is not an artifice, a scientific creation, a mechanical combination; society is a providential and indestructible phenomenon; men, like all animals that behave meekly, are social by nature. The state of nature is already a state of society; it is therefore absurd, when it's not scandalous, to wish to constitute, by a contract, that which is constituted of itself and by necessity. In second place, because my social mode of being, my employment, my belief, by views, my affections, my tastes, my interests, my habits escape the apprehensibility of every stipulation; for the simple, but prior reason, that all that I have enumerated is variable and indeterminate; because what I work at might change tomorrow; because my beliefs, my views, my affections, my tastes, my interests, my habits change, either every year, or every month, or every day, or many times per day, and I'm not happy to commit myself vis-à-vis anything, either by word, or by writing, never to change either employment, or belief, or views, or affection, or tastes, or interests, or habits; declaring that if I took on such a commitment I would only break it, if it were made under compulsion, it would be the most barbaric and the most odious of all tyrannies.

However, our social life is governed by contracts. Rousseau invented the whole thing, and for the past sixty years the genius of Rousseau has lurked in our legislation. It's by virtue of a contract, written by our fathers and lately renewed by the great citizens of the Constituent, that the government orders us not to look at, not to listen to, not to speak, not to write, not to do anything but what it allows us to do. These are the popular prerogatives whose alienation constitutes the government of men; as for this government, I question it as to what concerns me, leaving it to others to serve it, pay it, love it, and ultimately to die for it. But even if the entire French people consented to be voluntarily governed in its education, its worship, its credit, its employment, its art, its work, its affection, its tastes, is habits, its movements, and even its food, I declare that, by right, its voluntary slavery no more commits my own responsibility than its stupidity compromises my own intelligence; and if its servitude actually extends over me without any possible way to escape it; if it is beyond argument, which I can't doubt, that the submission of six, seven or eight million individuals to one or many men implies my own submission to this same man or to these same men, I defy anyone to find in this act anything but an ambush, and I affirm that at no time has the barbarity of any people brought to Earth a more aptly named brigandry. Even, indeed, a moral coalition of eight million lackeys for every single free man is a spectacle of cowardice against whose savagery civilization can't be invoked without making it look ridiculous or odious to everyone.

But I simply can't believe that all my compatriots intentionally feel the need to serve. What I feel must also be felt by everyone; for I am neither more nor less than just another man; I'm in the same simple and toilsome conditions of any other worker. I'm shocked, I'm terrified to meet at every step I take in life, at every thought I welcome into my head, at every enterprise that I embark upon, at every dollar I need to earn, a law or a regiment telling me: *One doesn't pass this way, one doesn't think that way; one doesn't undertake this; half this dollar will be left here.* To these many obstacles, which arise on all sides, my intimidated mind slouches towards stupor; — I don't know where to turn; I don't know what to do, I don't know what to become.

Who then has added to the atmospheric scourges, to the decompositions of the air, to the unhealthiness of the climate, to the thunder which science has tamed, this occult and savage power, this wicked genius that awaits humanity in the crib, only to have it devoured by humanity? Who indeed? Well, it's only men who, lacking enough hostility from the elements, have also taken each other as enemies.

The masses, still too docile, are innocent of all the brutality that is committed in their name and to their detriment; they are innocent, but not ignorant; I believe that, like me, they sense it and are outraged by it; I think that, like me, they feel pressed to get rid of it; only, failing to disentangle all the causes, they don't know what to do. I will try to establish both things for them.

Let's begin by pointing out the guilty parties.

ON THE ATTITUDE OF THE PARTIES AND THEIR JOURNALS

The majesty of the People has no organ in the French press. Papers for the bourgeois, papers for nobles, papers for the priesthood, republican papers, socialist papers: So much livery! Pure domesticity. All these rags polish, rub, dust the harness of some political knight in anticipation of a tournament, the prize of which is power, the prize of which is, consequently, my servitude, the servitude of the People.

With the exception of *La Presse* which, often, when its editor forgets his arrogance in favor of pride, manages to summon some elevated sentiment; and *La Voix du Peuple*[11] which, from time to time, departs from its old routines to cast some light on things of general interest, I can't read a French daily without feeling, for its writers, great pity or deep contempt.

On one hand, I see this governmental journalism on its way in, the journalism that is powerful thanks to the budget's gold and the army's steel, with a head encircled by the investiture of the supreme authority, and holds in its hand the thunderbolts consecrated by this investiture. I see it coming, I say, with fire in its eye, foam on its lips, fists clenched like a king of the marketplace, like some hero of the boxing ring; shouting with ease and with a brutal cowardice at his disarmed opponent whom he can abuse as he likes, and from whom he has nothing, absolutely nothing to fear; calling him a thief, a murderer, an arsonist; confining him

---

[11] (Translator): This was Proudhon's paper.

like a wild animal, refusing him any pittance, casting him into prisons without knowing how, without saying why and congratulating himself for it, boasting of his glory, as if, by fighting unarmed people, he had anything to lose or ran any risk.

This cowardice is disgusting.

On the other hand, there is the opposition journalism, the grotesque and ill-bred slave; passing its time moaning, whining and asking for mercy; saying each time it's spit on, with each blow given to it: *You mistreat me, you are unfair, I haven't done anything to bother you*; and arguing stupidly, as if to legitimize the invectives addressed to him: *I'm not a thief, I'm not a murderer, I'm not an arsonist; I venerate religion, I love the family, I respect property; you're the one who brings all these things into contempt. I'm better than you and you're oppressing me! You're not fair.*

This baseness is outrageous!

Against polemicists like those I find in the opposition, I grasp the brutality of power; I understand it, for, after all, when the weak party is abject, its weakness can be overlooked, only its abjectness is thought of; abjectness is irritating, like everything that crawls and is trampled underfoot like a worm. What I fail to understand in a group of men who call themselves democrats and who speak in the name of the People, the principle of all greatness and all dignity is abjectness.

He who speaks in the name of the people speaks in the name of the law; but I fail to understand how the law is irritated, nor do I see how it deigns to argue with error, with all the more reason should I fail to comprehend how it can stoop to complaining and begging. We suffer oppression, but we don't argue with it when we wish it dead; for to argue is to compromise.

Power is instituted; you give yourself a master; you are set (the whole country, by your adorable advice and your initiative, has been set) at the disposition of a few men; these men use the power you have given them; they use it against you, and you complain?

Why?

Did you think they would use it against themselves?

You can't have thought that; who is to blame, then?

Power must necessarily be wielded for the benefit of those who have it and to the detriment of those who don't have it; it is not possible to set it in motion without harming some and favoring others.

What would you do if it were invested in you?

Either you wouldn't use it at all, which would be to purely and simply renounce its investiture; or you would use it for your benefit and to the detriment of those who now have it and who no longer had it; then you would cease to moan, whine and beg to assume the role of those who insult you and transfer yours to them; but what makes me, O People, who has never had power and who makes it anyway; me, who pays the oppressor with blood and silver, whoever he may be and wherever he may come from, and who am still oppressed no matter how things turn out; what gives me this seesaw which, by turns, debases and exalts cowardice and abjectness?

What should I say about the government and the opposition, but that the former is a tyranny in reserve, and that the latter is a tyranny on the battlefield?

And why should I despise this champion more than the other, when both only want to build their pleasures and their fortunes on my pain and my ruin?

POWER IS THE ENEMY

There's not a single journal in France which doesn't cover a party, there is no party which doesn't aspire to power, there is no power which isn't the enemy of the People.

There is no newspaper that doesn't incubate a party, for none of them rises to this level of popular dignity, where the calm and supreme contempt of sovereignty has its throne; the People is impassive as the law, proud as force, noble as liberty, the parties are turbulent as error, aggressive as impotence, vile as servility.

There is no party which doesn't aspire to power, for a party is political by essence and forms, consequently, the very essence of power, the source of all politics. And if a party ceased to be political, it would cease to be a party and would blend back in with the population, that is, to the order of interests, of production, of industry and business.

There is no power which is not the enemy of the people, for whatever conditions it finds itself in, whomever it is invested in, whatever his name may be, power is always power, i.e., the unquestionable sign of the abdication of the sovereignty of the people, the consecration of a supreme mastery.

And the master is the enemy. La Fontaine said it first.

Power is the enemy, in the social order and the political order.

In the social order:

For the agricultural industry, the nursing mother of all the national industries, is crushed under the taxation by which power strikes it, and devoured by the usury disastrously levied by the financial monopoly, the exercise of which is guaranteed by power to its disciples or agents;

For labor, that is, intelligence, is confiscated by power, aided by its bayonets, for the benefit of capital, an element that is crude and stupid in itself, which would logically be the lever of industry if power brought no obstacles to their mutual association, and instead snuffs it out, thanks to power which separates the two, which only pays it half and, if it doesn't pay at all, for its use, for the laws and tribunals of governmental institution, which are ready to postpone for many years the satisfaction of the offended laborer's appetite;

Because commerce, muzzled by the monopoly of the banks, to which power holds the key, and garroted by the slipknot of a turpid regulation, the end of which is held by power, can, in virtue of a contradiction that would be a certificate of idiocy if it existed anywhere but with the most intellectual people on Earth, fraudulently enrich itself indirectly on the backs of women and children, while it's prohibited from ruining itself on pain of notoriety:

Because education is curtailed, chiseled at, gnawed on and reduced to the narrow dimensions of the mold confected for this purpose by power, such that all intelligence which has not been stamped by the power is as good as nonexistent;

Because those who fund, via power, the temples, the churches and synagogues, are the very same people who never go to the temples, the churches or the synagogues;

Because, to keep it brief, he is criminalized who hears, sees, says, writes, feels, thinks, acts differently from what power tells him to hear, see, say, write, feel, think, do.

In the political order:

Because the parties only exist and only soak the country in blood by and for power.

It isn't Jacobinism that the legitimists, the Orléanists, the Bonapartists, the moderates fear, it's the power of the Jacobins;

It isn't against legitimism that the Jacobins, the Orléanists, the Bonapartists, the moderates wage war, it's against the power of the legitimists.

And reciprocally.

All the parties you see moving on the surface of the land, like the foam floating on some boiling matter, have not declared war because of their differences in doctrine or views, but because of their common aspirations to power; if each of these parties could confidently state that the power of any of their opponents wouldn't bother it, the antagonism would instantly vanish, the way it ceased, 24 February 1848, when the people had devoured the power and the parties were assimilated.

It is therefore true that a party, whichever it may be, only exists and is only feared because it aspires to power; it is, therefore, true that none are dangerous which aren't in power; it is true, consequently, that whoever is in power suddenly becomes dangerous; it is, on the other hand, superabundantly established that be no public enemy except power.

Therefore, socially and politically speaking, power is the enemy.

And, since I've shown above that there are no parties that don't aspire to power, it follows that all parties are premeditatedly the enemy of the people.

THAT THE PEOPLE ONLY WASTES ITS TIME AND PROLONGS ITS SUFFERINGS BY ESPOUSING THE QUARRELS OF THE GOVERNMENTS AND PARTIES

This is the explanation for the absence of all the people's virtues in the heart of the governments and the parties; this is how, in these groups that feed on petty hatreds, miserable rancor, minute ambitions, the attack is cowardly and the defense is abject.

The old journalism must be crushed; these masters without a trace of nobility, who quiver at the thought of becoming lackeys, must be rendered destitute; these lackeys without a trace of pride, who lie in wait for the moment they'll become masters, must be dismissed.

To understand the urgency of killing off the old journalism, it is necessary for the people to see two things clearly.

Firstly, that it only neglects its business and prolongs it suffering by espousing the quarrels of the governments and the parties, by directing its activity towards politics instead of applying it to its material interests.

Secondly, that nothing can be expected from any government or any party.

Although I'll demonstrate this more precisely later, I will here state as a fact that a party, robbed of this patriotic state and the prestige with which it surrounds itself to ensnare the idiots, is quite simply nothing but a collection of vulgar power-hungry men, hunting for jobs. That is so true that the Republic only seemed tolerable to the royalists from the moment when the public functions were filled by the royalists who, I swear, will never seek to restore the royalty if only they could peacefully occupy all the good posts in the Republic. That is so true that the republicans found royalism tolerable from the moment when, in the name of the Republic, they managed and administered it. That is, finally, so true that the bourgeois party waged war from 1815 to 1833 on the nobles, since the bourgeois were taken out of the jobs; that the nobles and the republicans waged war from 1830 to 1848 on the bourgeois, because both of them had been removed from their positions and since, after the royalists came to power, the main grievance against them is that they dismissed the bureaucrats with self-proclaimed republican education, thereby confirming, with touching naivety, that, for them, the Republic is just about getting paid.

For the same reason that a party is set in motion in order to grab jobs or power, the government, which is enriched by it, agitates to keep them. But, as a government finds itself, rightly or wrongly, surrounded by an apparatus of forces which allows it to hunt, to persecute, to oppress those who would dispossess it, the people who, as a result, endure the oppressive measures provoked by the agitation of the ambitious, and whose magnanimity, besides, is sensitive to the tribulations of the oppressed, suspends its business, sets a period in the path it's on, informs itself of what's said, of what's done, gets heated up, irritated and finally lends a hand to help take down the oppressor.

But, since the people doesn't fight for itself, since the law, as I'll explain later, doesn't need to fight in order to win, it triumphs without benefit; placed in the service of the ambitious, its arm has ushered into power a new coterie in place of the old one, and soon the oppressors from the old one, now the oppressed, the people who, as before, again receives the backlash from the oppressive measures provoked by the agitation of the defeated party and whose magnanimity, as always, is sensitive to the tribulations of the victims, again suspends its business, and ultimately lends its support once again to the ambitious.

But one thing is for sure, in this brutal and cruel game, the people does nothing but waste its time and worsen its own situation; it is impoverished and suffers. It doesn't move a single inch forward.

It is hard, I'll freely confess, for the popular fractions which are all feeling, all passion, to contain themselves when the needling of tyranny pricks them too hard; but it is established that the enthusiasm of the parties only tends to make matters worse, it's also been shown that the miseries the people complains of is brought to it by groups which, since they don't act like it, are acting against it, all that remains for the parties is to halt, in the name of the people they oppress, it's up to the parties to call a halt, in the name of the people they oppress, impoverish, those they stupefy and accustom to do nothing but quarrel. But there is no counting on the parties. The people should only count on itself.

Without going further back in our history, taking only the pages of the two past years that have just gone by, it is easy to see that all the oppressive laws which have been made were originally caused by the turbulence of the parties. It would be long-winded and fastidious to enumerate them all here, but I should say, to stick precisely to the historical facts, that if, after February 1848, a tyrannical measure can be cited which is based on nothing but party provocations, which are due to the good pleasure of power, this is what Ledru-Rollin ordered, in his circulars, his prefects to do.

Ever since this epoch, the popular prerogatives have vanished one by one, having been discovered and handed over by the impatience and agitation of the ambitious. Since power was unable to specialize, the law strikes everyone with the blows that the parties alone should suffer, the people is oppressed, the fault lies only with the parties.

If the parties didn't feel the people at their backs, if, at very least, the people, exclusively concerned about its material interests, its professions, its trade, its business, covered with its indifference or even its contempt this base strategy which is called politics, if it assumed, with respect to moral agitation, the attitude it took on June 13 vis-à-vis the material agitation, the parties, suddenly isolated, would cease to agitate; the feeling of their impotence would freeze their audacity; they would dry up on the spot, would gradually be dispersed among the people, would finally vanish and the government which only exists by opposition, which only feeds on the quarrels that the parties stir up, which has its *raison d'être* only in the parties, which, in brief, for the past fifty years has done nothing but defend itself and which, if it no longer defended itself, would cease to be, the government, I say, would rot away like a dead body; it would dissolve of itself, and liberty would find a foundation.

THAT THE PEOPLE CAN EXPECT NOTHING FROM ANY PARTY

But the disappearance of the government, the annihilation of the governmental institution, the triumph of the liberty of which all the parties speak, will really not be the business of any party, for I've abundantly proven that a party, by the mere fact of being a party, is essentially governmental. Thus, the parties carefully keep the people from believing that they can do without government. Their daily polemics do, indeed, show that the government acts badly, that its policies are bad, but that it could do better, that its policies could be better. Ultimately, every journalist leaves this idea at the core of his articles: *if I were there, you'd see how well I'd govern!*

Fine, then! Let's see if there truly is a fair way to govern; let's see if it's possible to establish a government that's a driven guide, a power, an authority on the democratic basis of respect for the individual. I intend to get to the bottom of this question, for I've already said that the people could expect nothing from any government or any party, and I'm in a hurry to show my proofs.

Here we are in 1852; the power you hope to have, you who are part of the Montagne faction, you socialists, you *moderates* even — I don't have it — you have it. The left has an imposing majority, congratulations; you're welcome. Compliments out of the way, how do you intend to get to work?

I forgive your internal divisions; I'll overlook men like Girardin, Proudhon, Louis Blanc, Pierre Leroux, Considérant, Cabet, Raspail or their disciples among you; I'll assume that a perfect unity prevails among you, for your benefit I'll assume the impossible, for I would, before all else, facilitate the argument.

So you're all harmony then, what will you do now?

The release of all political prisoners; a general amnesty. Fine. You won't make an exception, surely, for the princes, for you will act as if you fear them and this fear will betray a mistrust of yourselves; this will be a confession that they might be preferred over you, a confession that would imply your uncertainty about realizing the general good.

With injustice sorted out in the political order, let's take a look at the economy and sociability.

You won't go bankrupt, that goes without saying, you're the ones who raised the objection against Mr. Fould; the national honor that you understood like "Garnier-45 centimes"[12] will require you to respect the stock exchange to the detriment of thirty-five million taxpayers; the debt created by the monarchies has too noble a character for the whole French people not to be bled annually of four hundred fifty million annually for the benefit of a handful of

---

[12] Translator: A nickname given to the minister of Finance, Louis-Antoine Garnier-Pagès (1803-78) because of an unpopular tax he supported.

speculators. You will begin, then, by saving the debt, we will be ruined but reputable, these two labels don't match our times well at all; but, finally, it's already long since you've done so, and the people, swamped by debt, as before, will think whatever it likes about it.

But, I think, you should first relieve the poor, the workers, the proletariat; you arrive with a law on taxation of the rich. And just in time, too! I'm a capitalist and you demand one percent, by God! Whatever will I do? Come to think of it, it isn't me who uses my capital, I lend it to industry; the industrialist, with his great need for it, won't fail to take one for an additional one percent, so I'll get my contribution. The tax on capital clearly falls on the nose of labor.

I'm a rentier and you hit the public bonds, for example, which is worrying. All things considered, however, there is a way out. Who is the debtor? The State. Since it's the State, things aren't so bad; the tax on the bonds immediately devalues these bonds to the same amount; the bonds, depreciated to the detriment of the debtor, which is the State, and to the benefit of the treasurer, which is the State; the State takes from its pocket to add to its bank and it's even, and so am I. The trick is a neat one, and I confess you're really something.

I'm the proprietor of houses in the city and you tax my apartments; to this I have nothing, absolutely nothing to say. You come to an agreement with my tenants; for you surely don't suppose I'm stupid enough not to cover this tax by raising the rent.

The most senseless phrase that has been uttered since the February revolution is this one: TAX THE RICH! Which is, if not perverse, at least deeply unreflective. I don't know who we call rich in a country like ours, where everyone is in debt and where the state of morals leads most of the proprietors, rentiers and capitalists, to spend, in any given year, more than they make. In any case, granting the existence of the rich man, I defy you to lay hold of him, your attempts will only show a gross ignorance of the elementary laws of social economy and the solidarity of interests. Your intended attack on the rich will impact the industrialists, the proletarians, and the poor. Would you relieve the poor? Then don't tax anyone. Administer France with 180 or 200 million, as they do in the United States; for 200 million in a country like France can be raised without anyone noticing; don't we give a hundred only to smoke bad cigars?

But, for that, administration is all that's needed, while you wish to govern: which is a very different thing. So, go ahead and attack the rich, after which you will settle your accounts with the poor.

Already, the formation of your budget saddles you with many malcontents; these questions of cash, you see, are quite delicate. Finally, let's forget about them.

Do you proclaim the unrestricted freedom of the press? That won't be allowed. You won't change the basis of the tax system; you won't touch the public wealth without making yourself vulnerable to the sort of discussion that will leave you less than spry. I don't personally feel disposed to prove, clear as day, your incompetence on this point and your own preservation would mean silencing me, besides, you would do well to do so.

The press won't be free, then, thanks to the budget. No government with a large budget can proclaim the freedom of the press; this is expressly forbidden for it. Promises won't be in short supply; but making a promise isn't the same as keeping it, just ask Mr. Bonaparte.

You will obviously keep the ministry of public education and the monopoly on universities; except that you'll exclusively guide the teaching in a philosophical direction, declaring savage war on the clergy and the Jesuits, which will make me a Jesuit just to oppose you, as I became a philosopher against Mr. de Montalembert, in the name of my liberty, which consists in being what I like, without either you or the Jesuits having anything to do with it.

And what about religion, will you abolish the Ministry of Religion? I doubt it. I imagine that, to help all the governomaniacs, you would rather create ministries than get rid of them. There will be a Department of Religion as there is today, and I'll end up paying the salaries of the parish priest, the minister and the rabbi because I neither go to the mass, the sermon, or communion.

You'll keep the Department of Commerce, that of Agriculture, that of the Public Works, that of the Interior, above all, for you would have prefects, sub-prefects, state police, etc., and by retaining and managing all these ministries, which are the very definition of today's tyranny; but this won't keep you from saying that the press, education, religion, commerce, public works, agriculture are all free. But they say the same thing right now. What would you do that isn't now being done? I'll tell you what you would do: instead of attacking them, you would defend them.

I see no way for you but to change the entire staff of the administrations and offices, and to treat the reactionaries just as the reactionaries treat you. But this is not called governing, is this system of retaliation really what government is? Judging by what has happened for some sixty years now, if I take note only of what you have to do while becoming a government, I have to say that governing is nothing but fighting, avenging, punishing. But, if you can't see that you're actually fighting on our backs and hitting your opponents, we can't for our part, hide it and I think the spectacle must come to an end.

To sum up all the powerlessness of a government, any at all, to bring welfare to the public, I'll just say this: that no good can come from anything but reforms. And, since every reform is necessarily a liberty, and all liberty is a force gained by the people, and, on the other hand, an attack on the integrity of power, it follows that the way of reforms which, for the people, is the way to liberty, is, for power, nothing but the disastrous path of decline. If, then, you say that you want power to carry out the reforms, you would also be confessing that you want to attain power with the premeditated goal of abdicating power. Aside from the fact that I'm not stupid enough to think you're that smart, I find that it would be contrary to all laws, whether natural or social, and principally that of self-preservation, which no creature can neglect, for men invested with the public power to consciously and willingly give away, both the investiture of it and the princely right it gives them to live in luxury without being worn out by its production. Go spread your nonsense somewhere else.

Your government can have only one object: to avenge you for the present one, just as the one that follows you can have only one aim: to get revenge on you. Industry, production, commerce, the affairs of the people, the interests of the multitude are unsuited to these fighting matches; I suggest you be left alone to dislocate your jaws while we go about our business.

If French journalism would be worthy of the people it addresses, it should cease to quibble over the deplorable loins of politics. Let the rhetoricians fabricate the laws as they like, which interests and customs will overrun, when it pleases you not to interrupt, with your futile outcries, the free development of the interests and the manifestation of the customs. Politics has never taught anyone how to honorably earn their dinner; its precepts have only ever served to pay for idleness and encourage vice. Let's leave off talking politics, then. Fill your columns with economic and commercial studies; tell us about some useful inventions; about things that, anywhere on Earth, have been discovered as materially or morally profitable for the growth of production, the improvement of well-being; keep us up to date on industrial development, so that we might, with this information, have the means of making a living and situating our lives in a comfortable environment. All these things are more important for us, I say, than your stupid dissertations on the balance of powers and on the violation of a

Constitution which, even if it had kept its virginity, wouldn't seem to me, to speak frankly, very worthy of my respect.

ON THE POLITICAL ELECTORATE, OR UNIVERSAL SUFFRAGE

I am naturally led, by what has been said, to the examination of the causes which produce the vices of which I've spoken. I discover these causes in the electorate.

It's two years now since, for sordid reasons, which I would like to believe that the parties haven't noticed, the people have been kept in the belief that it will never achieve sovereignty, welfare, without the aid and intercession of regularly elected representatives.

The vote, — a municipal thesis of its own, — can guide the people to liberty, to sovereignty, to welfare, in exactly the same way as giving everything away can lead a man to wealth. By which I mean that the exercise of universal suffrage, far from being a guarantee, is only the pure and simple surrender of sovereignty.

The electorate, of which the pedants of the last Revolution have spoken so much and with such gravity, the electorate, placed ahead of liberty, like the fruit before the flower, or the conclusion before the principle, or rights before facts, is the most solemn platitude that has ever been imagined at any time or in any country. Not only those who have allowed themselves, those who have been audacious enough to call the people to vote before allowing it to stabilize itself in its freedom, have grossly abused their inexperience and fearful docility which was imprinted on its character by a lengthy state of dependency; but they have also, by giving orders to the sovereign and by declaring themselves, by this alone, superior to it, misunderstood the basic rules of logic, which ignorance should have brought them down, as victims of their abnormal invention, and depart, pressed by the outcome of universal suffrage, to wander sadly in exile.

A strange thing, something to which I should draw the reader's attention, from the outset, for the sake of the demonstration that will follow: that it's for the benefit of the group formed by all the henchmen of the monarchies, universal suffrage has ended up benefiting the declared enemies of universal suffrage. The people has said thanks to those who confined it; it gave them, by voting, the right they take advantage of, to hunt it with nets and lures, watching and running, free-shooting or trapping, with the law as its weapon and their peers as hounds.

Certainly, in presence of the sort of thing that devours those who gave birth to it, and which renders all-powerful those who have tortured it in utero, it's certainly permissible, I think, to refuse to blindly accept this supposed palladium of democracy, which is called the electorate or universal suffrage. I even take it upon me to declare that I fight against it, like something evil, an outsized monstrosity.

The reader will already have realized that this is a case, not of contesting a right of the people's, but of correcting a disastrous error. The people has all imaginable rights; for my part, I attribute myself every right, even that of blowing my brains out or jumping in the river; but, aside from the fact that the right to my own destruction resides outside the calm of the natural law and ceases to call itself a right by becoming an anomaly from rights, a despair, this abnormal exaltation which, to help the argument, I'll also refer to as a right, cannot, in any case, give me the faculty of sharing with my fellows the fate that is appropriate for me, personally, to endure. Is it the same with the right to vote? No. In this case, the fate of the voter impacts the fate of he who abstains.

I stubbornly persist in my belief that the voters don't know that they are committing civic and social suicide by going to vote; an old prejudice still keeps them far from themselves, and their habit of being with the government keeps them from seeing that they should instead be with themselves. But by assuming that, impossible as it may be, the voters who leave their business, who neglect their most pressing interests to go and vote, had a strong sense of this truth, that is: that they are robbing themselves, by the vote, of their freedom, of their sovereignty, of their wealth in favor of their electees who, henceforward, are substituted for themselves; by supposing that they know this and that they freely but insanely consent to remain dependent on their mandatary, I fail to see how their own alienation should drag that of their fellows with them. I fail to see, for example, how or why the three million Frenchmen who never vote can escape the legal or arbitrary oppression brought to bear by a government fabricated by the seven million who do vote. I fail to see, in a word, how a government which I never made, which I couldn't have wished to make, which I would never consent to make, can come and demand my obedience and money, on the pretext that its authors have authorized it to do so. This is obviously a trap which requires an explanation, which I will provide. But first I will make room for the following reflection which is suggested to me by the electoral events of the 28th of this month.

When I got it into my head to publish this journal, I didn't select my day, or think about the election in preparation; my convictions lead me too high for them ever to become the humble servants of circumstances and eventualities. In addition, by supposing that the effect of the exposé given hereafter might be harmful to some party — a very gratuitous supposition, to be sure, — one voice more or less on the right or left wouldn't change the parliamentary situation. And if, after all, the parliamentary system completely crumbled at the impact of my arguments, this would do even less to keep me from disregarding precisely what, as will have been guessed, is the system I'm fighting against.

In addition, it's far less important to know whether I'm upsetting the fanatics of universal suffrage or their exploiters, than to be sure whether my doctrines are based on universal reason; but I am, as for the last point, completely at ease; and I dare say that, were I not saved by the obscurity of my name from the attacks of those who feed upon the voting public, I would still find, in the soundness of my deductions, refuge where their own prudence would prohibit them from coming to look for me.

The parties will receive this journal with contempt; this, in my opinion, is the wisest thing they could do. They would have to respect it too much if they didn't look down on it.

This journal is not the journal of a man, it is the journal of MAN or it is nothing.

THAT THE ELECTORATE IS NOT AND CANNOT BE ANYTHING BUT A DUPERY AND A DESPOLIATION

That said, I will approach the question and, without worrying about any feelings of fear or any dreams of hope that might be urged on me, now by the evokers of monarchy, and now the prophets of dictatorship. Using the inalienable faculty bestowed by my title of citizen and my interests as a man, reasoning dispassionately and without weakness; austere as my right, calm as my thoughts, I will say:

Every individual who, in the present state of things, drops into the ballot box a political slip for the election of a legislative power or an executive power is, if not voluntarily, at least unwittingly, if not directly, at least indirectly, a bad citizen.

I maintain this without retracting a syllable.

With things formulated in this way, I'm suddenly free of the royalists who pursue the realization of the electoral monopoly, and of the republican governmentalists, who make the formation of political powers into product of the common law, I actually fall, not into isolation, which in fact wouldn't bother me, but into the center of this vast democratic knot — more than a third of registered voters — who protest, by continual abstention, against the unworthy and miserable condition that has, for the past two years, caused the deleterious ambition and the no less deleterious deception of both parties and onlookers.

Among 353,000 voters registered in the département of the Seine, only 260,000 participated in the vote of last March 10th; those who abstained were even more numerous this time than in previous elections. Paris, as a more intense political center than other ones and which therefore contains fewer indifferent men than the countryside; we can truly say that the political powers are formed without the participation of more than a third of the citizens of the land. And I'm with this third; for with it, you must agree, one finds neither the fear-based voting on the pretext of preservation, nor ambition, which votes only to conquer, nor the sheeplike ignorance that votes for the sake of voting; here we see philosophical serenity, useful work with a placid conscience, uninterrupted production, merit without fame, modest courage.

The parties call these wise and serious philosophers of material interests, who didn't take part in the saturnalia of scheming, bad citizens; the parties abhor political inertia, metal without pores where domination cannot find purchase. It is time to take notice of these legionaries of abstention, the stability of democracy is found there; with them resides liberty, so exclusively, so absolutely, that this liberty won't be acquired by the nation until the day when the whole population imitates their example.

To elucidate this demonstration, two things need to be examined:

Firstly, what is the object of the political vote?

Secondly, what must its result inevitably be?

The political vote has a dual aim: one direct, one indirect. The first aim of the political vote is to constitute a power; the second is — with the power in place — to make the citizens free and to reduce their burdens; besides, this is only to treat them justly.

This is, unless I'm mistaken, the avowed object of the political vote, as to the interior. The exterior is not in question here.

Already, then, by going to vote, and by the mere fact of voting, the voter admits that he is not free, and he grants his electee the ability to give it to him; he admits that he has a burden, and he admits that the elected power has the power to remove it; he declares himself in favor of the establishment of justice and he concedes to his delegate all authority to judge him.

Very well. But, isn't the recognition that one or many men have the power to set me free, to unburden and judge me, to place my liberty, my wealth, my rights outside of myself? Is this not a formal confession that this man or these men who can liberate me, unburden me, judge me, are not only able to oppress me, ruin me, misjudge me, but also that they are incapable of doing otherwise, since, by replacing all my rights with these men, I no longer have any rights, and that, to protect all rights, they only need to protect themselves?

If I ask someone for something, I accept that this person has what I'm asking them for; it would be absurd for me to petition for something I already have. If I had use of my liberty, of my fortune, of my rights, I wouldn't ask power for them. And, if I ask them from power, it's probably because it has possession of them, and, if it has them, I can't see why it would care about anything I might teach it about how to use them.

But how has power come into possession of what belongs to me? Who did it come from? Power, taking as an example the one before us, is composed of Bonaparte who, just yesterday, was a poor outcast without too much freedom, and with no more money than freedom.

Some seven hundred fifty thundering Jupiters, dressed no different than anyone else, and certainly no more attractive, were talking several months ago, with us and no better than us, I dare say; between seven and eight ministers and their derivatives, most of whom, before pulling on the tail of the budget, first pulled the devil's, just as stubbornly as any of the linear writers. How did yesterday's poor rabble become my masters today?

By whom were these gentlemen, if you please, given the power in whose bosom you have all freedom, all wealth, all justice? Who should be blamed for the persecutions, the impositions and the iniquities that make us all groan? The voters, obviously.

The Constituent which has begun to give us the dance; Louis Bonaparte who continued the instrumentation, and the legislature which came to support the orchestra, none of that came about by itself. No, it was all produced by the vote. With the voters lies the responsibility for what has taken place and what will follow. We take no responsibility for it, we democrats of work and abstention; look elsewhere for collusion with the oppressive laws, inquisitorial regulation, butchery, military executions, mass incarceration, forced movement, deportations, the immense crisis that crushes the country. Go, government-maniacs, beat your chest and prepare for the judgment of history! Our conscience is easy. It's already plenty that, as a phenomenon repellent to all logic, we have to endure a yoke that you alone made; it's already plenty that, along with yours, our liberty has fled; it's already plenty for you to have delivered, along with what was yours, what didn't belong to you, that which should be inviolable and sacred: the liberty and wealth of others!

PRIMOGENITURE AND THE FRENCH PEOPLE'S PORRIDGE

Now don't go thinking, abused bourgeois, ruined gentlemen, sacrificed proletariat, don't go thinking that what has happened might have been otherwise, if you had nominated Peter instead of nominating Paul, if your votes went for James instead of Francis. Vote however you like, you are surrendering yourselves, and whoever comes out on top, his success will sweep you away. You'll have to ask for everything from one or another of them; therefore, you'll have nothing left!

Besides, you need to realize this — it's not science, it's truth, pure and simple, — if the evil came only from the reactionaries, if revolutionaries could improve your lot, you would be extremely rich; for all the governments, since Robespierre and Marat — may God keep their souls — were revolutionary; this assembly you have before your eyes formed itself as a composite of revolutionaries. Nobody has been more revolutionary than Thiers, the warden of Notre Dame de Lorette; Mr. de Montalembert has pronounced speeches on absolute liberty that can't be beat. Berryer was a conspirator between 1830 and 1848; Bonaparte brought revolution in writing, by word and deed; I'm not talking about the Montagne, a cenacle that held in its hands, for many months, the governmental means to cover you with a dew of opulence. All men have made revolutions when they haven't made the government; but all men too, when they have made government, have compromised the Revolution. Even I, who am speaking to you, if you decided one day to bring me to the government and if, in a moment of forgetfulness or giddiness, instead of feeling pity or contempt for your stupidity, I accepted the title of receiver of the theft you perpetrate against yourselves, I swear to God I'd show you some fine stuff! Or haven't all the prior experiments already shown you well enough? You really are difficult!

You have recently formed a white government whose only object, — and you can hardly blame it — is to get rid of the reds. If you make a red government, its one object — and it will be funny when you accept this too, — will be to get rid of the whites. But the whites only take vengeance on the reds and the reds on the whites through prohibitive and oppressive laws; now, whom do these laws oppress? Those who are neither red, nor white, or who are, to their own detriment, now white and now red, the uninvolved multitude; to the extent that the people is lies murdered by all the club-blows dealt on its back it by the parties.

I'm not critiquing the government; it was made to govern, it governs, it puts its rights to use, and whatever it may do, I agree that it's only doing its duty. The vote, by granting it power, has informed it of these things: *the people is perverse, you're upright; it is carried off by passion, you practice moderation; it is stupid, you are intelligent.* The vote, which has told the present majority, the president of this place, will also say so (for it can say nothing more, nothing less) to any majority, to any president at all.

Therefore, by the vote, and whatever its result, the people places itself, body and goods, at the mercy of its elected officials for them to use and abuse their liberty and their wealth; since nobody has expressed any reservations, authority has no limits.

But what about decency? it's said; but what about discretion! but what about honor! ... Smoke and mirrors! You look at feelings when you should be looking at numbers; if you put your interests above conscience, you're giving without hope of a return; conscience is a safety valve.

Think for a moment about what you're doing. You surround a man like some relic; you kiss the hem of his garments; you acclaim him with deafening screams; you lavish gifts on him; you stuff his pockets with gold; you rob yourself, for his benefit, of all your riches; you tell him: *Be free above the free, opulent above the opulent, strong above the strong, righteous above the righteous*, and then you try to control the way he uses your gifts? You let yourself criticize this, disapprove of that, add up his expenses and ask him for an accounting? What sort of accounting do you expect him to give? Have you written up the invoice for all you gave him? Your accounting is mistaken? Then you have no certificate to use against him; the sheet you want to hand him isn't authoritative; nobody owes you anything!

Now cry, storm, threaten, it's wasted effort; your debtor is your master: bow down and move along.

In the Biblical stories, it's said that Esau sold his birthright for porridge. The French go one better, they give away their birthright and the porridge too.

WHAT PRODUCES GOVERNMENTS IS NOT WHAT SUSTAINS THEM

I will repeat here that I'm not questioning the right itself; what I'm questioning as unfitting is the present use of the law. I say that, before using the right I've been given to nominate my delegates, it is important for me to begin by making this sovereignty a reality, by establishing myself materially in the facts, by seeing all I should do personally and what attributions my delegates should be given. I should, in a word, establish myself before I found anything whatsoever. The institutions shouldn't be made by the laws, on the contrary, they should make the laws. First I institute myself, and then I will make laws.

We should not forget that the theory of divine right, from which we descend directly, emanates from a supposed priority that the government would have with respect to the People. All our history, all our legislation, are based on this monumental absurdity, that is, that the government is a precession of the people, that the people is a deduction from the government; that there was or that there might have been a government prior to the existence of any people. This, then, is what is confessed here: the annals of the world are chiseled in this muck of human intelligence. As long, then, as the government lasts, the notion of its priority will remain intact, the divine right will be perpetuated among us and the people, whose suffrage is set in the place of the ancient rite of coronation, will never be, whatever name it assumes, anything more than a subject.

The transition from theocracy to democracy cannot, in any case, come by the exercise of the electoral law, for this exercise aims directly at keeping the government from perishing, i.e., to maintain and even revive the principle of governmental priority. We must, to pass from one regime to another, determine a solution of continuity in the chain of delegation. We must, since it is fatally urged towards the respect for theocratic tradition, suspend the delegation and only take it back after having introduced the regular exercise of *self-government* into social reality. It's only after having made property a reality that I should rationally set a manager over my estate; if I put him there before presenting my titles, he might refuse to acknowledge me, and rightly so.

But here is what I mean to say: Unanimity is, on all questions and in all countries, impossible. However, since every government comes from voting, nothing less is required, to keep a government from being born, than unanimous abstention; for, assuming that nine million out of ten million abstained, a million voters would still be allowed to make a government, which the whole nation would have to obey; and there will always be at least a million people in France with an interest in making a government; therefore, the proposition is absurd.

I respond:

It isn't even necessary to find a million men to form a government; a hundred thousand, ten thousand, five hundred, one hundred, five individuals can do this, even a single citizen can constitute one. In 1830, Lafayette by himself made Louis-Philippe the king; and during the 18 years that followed this event, the parliamentary power was made, in a country of 35 million souls, by the mere participation of 200 thousand *censitaires*. No matter how restricted the number of citizens may be who participate in the creation of a government, what does it even matter? All I would point out here is that no government can live against the wishes of the national majorities.

Philosophy and, in its wake, a surer school, the school of experience and facts, have demonstrated, in an irrefutable manner, that the deeper reason for the existence of the governments was, not the material or electoral consent of the citizens of a country, but rather the public faith or interests, since faith and interests are one and the same thing.

The government currently on the perch owes itself to the electoral recreations of seven to eight million very obedient citizens, each of whom wasted, with utmost graciousness, two or three days of work, to seize the occasion of giving themselves, body and property, to men they don't know, but whom they have guaranteed five pieces of five francs per day in order to make their acquaintance. Does it seem to you that the legislative Assembly and Mr. Bonaparte would be more solidly established than were both the Chamber of Deputies of 1847, created by two hundred thousand *censitaires* only; and Louis-Philippe, created by a single man? Tell me if you think that a government made by a million or fewer, individuals can be more narrow minded, more de-popularized, more perplexed than one made by eight million individuals. Obviously you don't think this. There is no man here — and when I say man, I mean to say the opposite of a bureaucrat — who hasn't had his interests or his faith deeply attacked by the regimes that have been successively established since 1848; there isn't, consequently, any man who could congratulate himself for the result of his vote and who could believe that something worse, that the thing that exists, might have come from his abstention. You must, therefore, confess that you have, by the smaller end, wasted your time; and, unless it enters your speculations — speculations, in this case, that are truly quite strange — to constantly waste your time. I imagine you must be quite ready to sacrifice the ballot to more sustaining realities. Your discontent is already a very bad bet for power, but if your slip wasn't there to encourage it, it would be quite weak, and I doubt it could even hold its cards.

Unanimity in abstention is not, therefore, what is important to obtain; just as unanimity in voting isn't necessary to form a government; unanimity in inertia cannot be the essential condition for the acquisition of the anarchic order which is in the interest and, consequently, the honor of all Frenchmen to realize. There will always be plenty of bureaucrats, supernumeraries and aspirants; there will always be plenty of State rentiers and pensionaries of the Treasury to constitute an electoral personnel, but the number of Chinese who would gladly pay all these mandarins shrinks every day, and if nineteen remain, in the next two years, I say here and now that it won't be my fault.

Besides, — and since we must leave nothing unsaid, — what do you call universal suffrage?

A newspaper arrives, saying: *We must elevate citizen Gouvernard.*

Then another paper appears, objecting: *No, we must elevate citizen Guidane.*

Don't listen to my opponent, replies the first paper, *citizen Gouvernard is the only candidate we need, here's why, etc.*

Never believe what my opponent tells you, replies the second paper, *nobody but citizen Guidane will do, here's why, etc.*

In the meantime, there steps in the arena, up to now keeping a proud, Olympian reserve, a third newspaper, the mastodon of the species, which pronounces this sentence in a professorial manner: *Mr. Gouvernard must be elected.*

And Mr. Gouvernard was elected.

And you say that it's the people who carried out the election? I'll beg your goblets and your nutmeg[13] for permission to find this expression imprecise.

---

[13] (Translator): An apparent reference to "cups and balls" magic trick ("gobelets" in French).

Let this be said to settle my accounts with the form and without compromising my reservations as to the heart of things.

But I know the republicans, or the supposed citizens, who have great fear that, if allowed to vote, the people might bring back the royalty. These are certainly great republicans who have rendered, as they claim, remarkable services, services I affirm that neither you, nor I, have ever seen the least shadow of, whether in terms of money, freedom, dignity, or honor. In common parlance, which is the language I speak, the fear felt by these republicans expresses the affliction caused by the impossibility of their personal elevation. I might well be deflowering patriotism a bit, but what do you expect? I'm no poet, and in mathematics and history I've found that, without these republicans, royalty would have been dead and buried for sixty years already; that without these republicans, who have given the monarchy the signal service of restoring authority each time the people has sought to give it a shove, the French, myself included, would have been free for a long time now. The royalists, believe me, won't go far the day these republicans offer the excessive favor of ceasing to play royalists. The royalists, I assure you, will stop short when, instead of simply granting them the majority, we leave the entire electoral field to them.

What I'm saying seems strange, right? It is indeed strange; but the situation is also strange, and I'm not one of those who dress up new situations in the old rags that for half a century have cluttered all the hovels of revolutionary journalism.

TO UNMASK POLITICS IS TO KILL IT

I will explain, and, even if it means repeating myself, I'll pose this question here:

What is the voter saying by depositing his ballot in the box? With this act, the voter tells the candidate: I give you my liberty without restriction or reservation; I place at your disposition, I hand over to your discretion my intelligence, my means of action, my capital, my income, my work, all my wealth; I surrender my rights and my sovereignty to you. In addition, it is understood that the liberty, the intelligence, the means of action, the capital, the income, the professions, the wealth, the rights, the sovereignty of my children, of those near to me, of my fellow citizens, both the active and the passive ones, fall, with all that I transmit to you on my own account, into your hands. The entirety is presented to you to use as you like; my guarantee is your whim and nothing more.

This is the electoral contract. Argue, object, dispute, interpret, turn it every way, poetize, sentimentalize, you won't change anything about it. This is the contract. The same goes for all candidates; republican or royalist, the man who has himself elected is my master, I am his thing; all Frenchmen are his thing.

It remains, therefore, understood that the electorate consecrates both the alienation of what is one's own, and the alienation of what belongs to others. It is evident, then, that the vote is, on one hand, a deception, and on the other, an indelicacy, or frankly speaking, plunder.

The vote would never be anything but a universal deception if all the citizens had the vote, and if all the voters voted; for, in this case, they would all break even with respect to each other, since all would lose by the act of each, but if a single voter abstains or is kept from voting, the plunder begins. And if, among nine to ten million voters, three million abstain, — this number has been reached today, — and the dispossessed already form a large enough minority to be taken into account. The ancient notion of probity in power is now ragged; but note how the decadence of power is proportionate to the decaying of this notion.

Assuming half of the electorate stays home, the situation becomes grave for the voters and the government they'll have made; the political skepticism of fully half of the social body must visibly chafe against the older beliefs of the other half. And if we consider that intelligence or liberty, which are one and the same thing, will be found precisely on the side of calculated, motivated, intentional inertia, while on the side of the vote there is only sheeplike and traditional instinct, ignorance or abnegation, which amounts to the same thing, it will be easy to imagine what sort of prostration should, in such a state of affairs, defeat the old governmentalism. In fact, we have, at this very moment, reached this period: for, if four million voters haven't abstained yet, it isn't because they're proud of having voted. And, regret implies a sense of wrongdoing.

Now let us test the hypothesis. Let's assume that all the opponents of royalism, having bought into the modern notion that power cannot be moral, desert the polls, basing their desertion on the incontestable truth that the vote is both deception and plunder, and the royalists will suddenly lose all collaborators; outside of them, you will find none but people who are knowingly wronged. The electorate, having become a misdeed by the enlightenment of public opinion, this misdeed falls directly and utterly on them: the thieves are well known. Or rather, in a nod to common sense, let's say that there are no more thieves at all; for, when the question is reduced to these severe, but simple and, above all, true terms; when politics, when brought back down from its ancient and charlatan heights, returns to the crimes it has always secretly, but truly, inspired, the governmental fiction vanishes and human reality detaches itself from all the misunderstandings which have, to date, produced the struggle and the deplorable events that have been its effects.

Behold the revolution! Behold the calm, wise, rational reversal of the traditional notion! Behold the democratic substitution of the individual for the State, of interests for ideas. No perturbation, no shakeup can be produced in this majestic tearing asunder of the historical clouds; the Sun of liberty appears without any storms and everyone, enjoying their share of its generous rays, from now on walks in broad daylight and pursues their proper place in society, according to aptitude or intelligence.

To be free, you see, you only have to want it. Freedom, which we have stupidly been taught to expect as a gift from others, freedom is already in us, we ourselves are freedom. Neither rifles, nor barricades, nor agitation, nor fatigue, nor clubs, nor elections will win it for us, for this is all sheer debauchery. But freedom is righteous and is only obtained by hesitation, serenity and decency.

When you ask the government for freedom, the naivety of your request immediately teaches it that you have no idea what your rights are; your petition is the act of a subordinate, you're confessing your inferiority; you're recognizing its supremacy, and the government takes advantage of your ignorance and it treats you like a blind man, for you are all indeed blind.

Those who petition the government every day, in their pages, for immunities for you are, — while asking you to believe that they're trying to ruin and weaken it, — giving the government all its power and wealth, power and wealth that they want preserved, since they want to attain it one day, with your help, O people, as duped, misused, taunted, robbed, guided, tricked, yoked, burdened, thrashed by schemers and cretins who make you grin and bear it by flattering you, courting you like a powerful force, by lavishing pompous titles on you like some king of vaudeville and by thus exposing you, as the prince of sheds and jails, monarch of drudgery, sovereign of poverty, to the jeering laughs of everyone!

As for me, I have no reason to flatter you; for I don't want to take anything of yours, not even my share of your miseries and your shame. But I have to ask you, you in particular, not the government, that I don't know, that I don't want to know,

I have to ask you for my freedom which you have wrapped up in the gift you made of your own. I don't ask this as an imposition on you, since, if I would be free, you must be as well. Learn how to be free! All that is required for this is to stop elevating others above you. Distance yourself from politics, which eats the masses, and apply your efforts in business, which feeds and enriches them. Remember that wealth and freedom are in cahoots, just as servitude and indigence are in cahoots. Turn your back on the government and the parties, which are nothing but its trainbearers. Contempt kills governments, for fighting is what nourishes them. Finally, be the sovereign, who doesn't quibble with his people, and laugh at the ridiculous intrigues of white royalism and red governmentalism. No obstacle can resist its calm and progressive manifestation of your needs and your interests.

"As long as the sire de Tillac didn't know what he was," says a Gascon legend, "his superior badly mistreated him; but when Lady Jehanne, his wet-nurse, informed him about his titles and rank, the people of the château, the warden at their head, came to bow before him."

Let the people show its superiors that it is no longer ignorant; that it will no longer meddle in the quarrels of the antechamber, and its superiors will be silent, with a respectful attitude. It owes its own freedom to itself, to the world that lies in wait, to the children who are yet to be born.

The new politics in hesitation, in abstention, in civic inertia and in industrial activity; in other words, in the very negation of politics. I'll develop these propositions at greater length.

Let it suffice to say today that, if the republicans hadn't voted in the last general elections, there would have been no opposition in the Assembly, and if there hadn't been an opposition in the Assembly, there wouldn't have been, in fact, any Assembly at all. There would only have been a state of chaos between the Legitimists, the Orléanists, the Bonapartists who would all have been ruined by each other, with the help of scandals; all three would have fallen, at the hour of writing this, under the exhilarating boos and hisses of liberty.

CONCLUSION

Of all I've said, and I'll return soon, whether to fill in any gaps, or to improve on what I've said in this exposé, the end result is that the aim of political voting is the formation of a government; but, since I've shown that the formation of a government, and of the opposition that serves as its essential safeguard, is the consecration of an inevitable tyranny, the source of which is the spontaneous gift by the voters, to their elected officials, of their bodies and goods, as well as the bodies and goods of all the non-voters; it follows that, if the alienation of sovereignty weren't a folly, but a right, when he who alienates it only has control of his own portion of it, this act ceases to be a folly or a right and becomes plunder when it involves the brutal argument of the greater number, of assimilating the sovereignty of the minorities with the fate chosen for its own sovereignty.

I add that, since all government is necessarily a cause of antagonism, of discord, of butchery and destruction; he who, by voting, participates in the formation of a government is an artisan of civil war, a promoter of crises and, consequently, a bad citizen.

Here I can hear the republicans of bureaucratism cry out: "Treason!" This won't bother me, for I know them better than they know themselves. I have an old score, going back sixty years, to settle with them, and their bankruptcy, in which I'll be a trustee, is far from a graceful one.

I also hear the royalists and the imperialists asking whether there may be something to glean from the harvest I've pointed to; this doesn't bother me, since I know the true value of their shabby wares.

The future belongs neither to the former, nor the latter, thank God; and the royalty is only waiting for the last fingernail of dictatorship to fall before loses its remaining tooth.

I intend to tear out both claws and stumps from these ladies.

Here's to the three of us!

THE REVOLUTION

L'Anarchie, journal de l'ordre

No. 2

I

In theory, the Revolution is the development of well-being[14].

---

[14] "Notice by A. Bellegarrigue to No. 2.": The editor of *L'Anarchie*, by taking head-on a word with the help of which the politicians have intimidated and ransomed the population, has proposed two things:

First, to prove that ORDER is a popular and anti-governmental element. The best argument in support of this thesis is the fact that the monarchical papers openly salute civil war as Providential.

Secondly, to establish that the Revolution is purely and simply a question of business. The political indifference and skepticism in which the people are more and more interested; its evident disdain for political arguments, and its professed contempt for those who

In practice, the Revolution was only the extension of the disease.

The Revolution should enrich everyone: this is the IDEA.

The Revolution ruined everyone: this is the FACT.

Do you know why the reality of revolution turned out so discordant with the idea?

---

would command it, corroborate this opinion and show that the editor of *L'Anarchie* is in agreement with the public mood.

The royalist parties, historically and materially ruined, were not worth fighting; what is important to destroy today is the pretense of the new parties which, on the pretext of disinterring the royalty, want to inherit its power. *L'Anarchie* must, therefore, unmask the revolutionaries for the benefit of the Revolution.

The old journalism is on its way out, dishonored by the interests it has compromised, burdened with the imprecations of the masses, from whom it learned nothing, cursed by the civilization it has polluted.

The old journalism knows nothing either about finances, industry, commerce or practical philosophy; as the positive sciences are established, its imposing ignorance is shown and, within a few months, it will vanish, deeply ashamed.

When fictions are crushed by the facts, the controversists have nothing more to say.

Nothing is simpler: in theory, the revolution should happen of itself, i.e., each social interest should furnish its own part of the action; in practice, the Revolution was carried out by a handful of individuals and subject to the authority of a group of rhetoricians.

The essential genius of the Revolution is the acquisition of wealth; the dominant instinct of revolutionaries is hatred of the rich, and this is precisely why, by becoming rich, revolutionaries cease to be revolutionary. While everyone tries to enrich themselves by working and applying themselves, while everyone cries loudly for the calm which multiplies transactions and ceaselessly displaces wealth by mobilizing and developing it; while, in this way, the true Revolution, that of individual needs and interests, vigorously struggles against the obstacles and the dykes of the tyrannical regulation of the governments, the revolutionaries arrive, this fatal tribe which, for the single and sordid satisfaction they seek of replacing those men in power, who are already being overrun by the force of things, stop the flow of things, suspend the solemn manifestation of the public interests, paralyze the Revolution, muddle the legislative details which social realities had tried to get rid of, and consolidate the governmental mastery, which business had nearly subdued.

There are, truly, no worse counter-revolutionaries than revolutionaries; for no citizens are worse than the envious ones.

This is not the place for a detailed examination of the period of *the ambitious* between 1789 and 1848. I don't have enough time or space for such a retrospective review which would show that the European Revolution was put to a stop and that the European governments were consolidated by the doctrinaire revolutionaries, the most sinister sort of people who ever lived. Someday I'll write the history of these sixty years, and the reader will be shocked to see to what sort of dark joke the Western world owed more than half a century of ruinous troubles and bloody mystifications.

For the moment, limited to contemporary history, I would interrogate the event of 1848, which I would be even less willing to label a Revolution since, from my point of view, the Revolution must be the destruction, not of *a* government, but of *the* government, while the Revolution of 1848 was only the consolidation of what was supposed to have been destroyed, and of what indeed would be long gone today, if the movement of 24 February hadn't taken place. Still, I won't go so far as to say that this movement, accepted by the universality of the citizens, couldn't have been turned in favor of the Revolution; far from arguing in this way, I'll seek on the contrary to demonstrate that the heads of this movement only needed to convert its governmental character into a revolutionary, industrial or anarchic character, which are all the same thing.

II

In the final years of Louis-Philippe's reign, the Revolution, — by which I mean the development of all the interests, — had so undermined the government that it had cracks everywhere, and that, by its numerous fissures, badly repaired by the emergency laws, introduced, with continual streams, the current that would carry it away.

Education felt pressed by the regulation of the universities.

Religion balked under the yoke of the State.

Justice was ashamed of its political dealings.

Trade and industry, worn out by governmental oversight, was already looking for a way to free itself from the routine of regulations and from the financial monopoly.

Arts and literature cried out against a tyrannical protection which awarded prizes according to favor and incompetence, while keeping true merit from showing its face.

And, concurrently with all these elements of public life, agriculture, our common mother, cried out for tax relief, which could only be obtained by suppressing the various sections of the protectorate and the budgets allocated to this protectorate.

The manifestation of the public needs had made the abuses of the tutelage so obvious, the social eddies caused by the administrative dykes made the floating existences so heavy, the regulatory burdens formed such a formidable phalanx that Guizot, to prevent spillage, had been forced to buy, not only the parliamentary bed, but also and above all, the source of this Political river that carried the governmental nave; Louis-Philippe's minister himself had bought the electorate:

Official France was its own, from the *censitaire* to the lawmaker, from the base to the summit.

Having reached this highest point of political appropriation, the government finds itself cornered; the Revolution must necessarily have its revenge, I mean, the upsurge of interests must pull it down; running out of ways to escape the new encroachments, everything was seized, everything but the social country, the real France, the industrial ascendancy, the appetite for comfort. The Revolution, in a word.

But this inexpugnable and unconquerable opponent, in whose presence the government ultimately found itself; this natural enemy who pressed it from every direction, the Revolution, — this must be understood, — has never had, can never have a man's name.

They called it Mirabeau, it protested.

They called it Danton, it was outraged.

They called it Marat, it trembled.

They called it Robespierre, it roared.

In our days, it's been given the names of Ledru-Rollin, of Louis Blanc, of Raspail; note its reaction.

Wo to the man who makes himself the Revolution; for the Revolution is the people, and whoever is brazen enough to personify the people commits the greatest outrage history has ever witnessed!

The Revolution is the flux of interests: nobody can represent interests, they represent themselves, the intense strength of their persistent and calm manifestation is the only rational and possible revolutionary force. Nothing is more troubling, nothing is more ruinous than to see in the assemblies, in journalism or in the street, certain individuals boasting that they represent the interests of the people, and thereby localize the Revolution in a radius of a few square feet. Interest is a notion that springs from the need, the preferences and the aptitudes of each person; it is, therefore, a purely personal thing which can't be delegated; no one can realize any interests but their own. When one man steps up to another and says: *I'll look after your business*, it's clear that, since this proposition is political or non-guaranteed, the businessman will make his client's business his own.

Since interests are purely personal and only realizable by the individual, their revolutionary goal aims at liberty. So, can this liberty, requisite for the realization of interests, be publicly personified in one or multiple delegates? No, one can no more represent the freedom than the interests of others. Liberty is not a political principle, it is an individual reality: man is free according to what he loves; he sacrifices his freedom to his interests every day, and he is only truly free to the extent that he has the discretion not to be so.

In this way, nobody can pose as the representative of the liberty or the interests of another without instantly becoming an authority and, consequently, without being caught in the act of government.

By localizing, in this way, in an assembly, in a club, in a journal, in a public square, or behind a barricade, the interests and liberties which belong essentially to the public domain, the Revolution is localized, as I've already said, is nothing other than the flux of interests and liberty, and by localizing the Revolution, it has been castrated, neutralized.

And so, I'm right when I say that there are no worse counter-revolutionaries than revolutionaries.

III

The governmentalists of the monarchy and the Republic spoke in striking harmony to persuade the people that its fortune was in the hands of authority; the truth is precisely the opposite. Power only has what it takes from the people, and if the citizens believe that they need to begin by giving what they had to attain welfare, their common sense must have been profoundly disturbed.

True, the combination on offer inevitably blinds the populations by arousing their cruder instincts and stimulating their base passions.

Something needs to be done, say the monarchists, *the people is suffering: we'll look after it*. Here already the monarchists are posing as the Providence of the naked masses and naturally inducing a ferment of envy in these masses.

The rich don't care about you, cry the republicans, addressing the belittled population, *we'll force them to give you part of what they have!* See, here we have revolutionaries who agree with the monarchists and proclaim the Providence of the masses to them.

In this way, the republicans and monarchists both realize that wealth must remain immobile in a certain class of citizens and that all the rest of the population should live from charity; a shameful and degrading error which produced the right to work and to assistance, the inevitable counterpart of which is the monopolization of capital; for it is impossible for me to ask someone for the right to work. If I haven't already recognized that this other party has an immutable right to own what I work with and upon, it doesn't take much intelligence to grasp this: just basic common sense.

This error, which has divided the French nation into privileged and mendicants, is what led to the idea of localizing the Revolution and making it the prerogative of a doctrinaire sect. By denying that individual initiative has the ability to move and universalize wealth by multiplication, by turning within the narrow circle of existing capital funds without any intention of making more, while making the social question a matter of jealousy instead of emulation and courage, faith has been inculcated in governmental initiative in the distribution of welfare; hence the need for the government. But the more government the revolutionaries desire for the sake of redistribution, in other words to monopolize, the more government the monarchists also want in order to monopolize, in order words to redistribute. It's not possible to redistribute wealth without already being the master of said wealth; the distribution thereof is, therefore, monopoly from the start; from which it follows that citizen Barbés and Léon Faucher profess exactly the same doctrine. In this way, the consolidation of the government is due to the dual action of the royalists and the revolutionaries. And it must be known that, no matter who controls it, the government is the negation of the Revolution, for a very simple reason: the government is enforced monopoly. The greatest fanatic for redistribution will come to the government, which I defy him to redistribute. Consider this.

Nobody can govern without the assistance of wealth; wealth is to the government as columns to a building, as legs to an individual. As soon, therefore, as, on the pretext of helping the poor, an individual is pressed into the government, this individual, to keep the balance, needs the help of the rich. And how can he ever dream of dispossessing the rich for the benefit of the poor, since his own preservation resides in the complete retention, if not of the personnel, at least of the monopoly of finance?

It's therefore clear that, once the Revolution is restricted to the meager and wretched proportions of a simple displacement of individuals, of a change of proper nouns, it has gone off the rails; it has fallen into an abyss; the worst of abysses, that of envy, idleness and mendicancy.

If, during the period of the reign of Louis-Philippe, the revolutionaries had praised the industrial initiative of individuals, instead of developing the stupid theses of State munificence; if they had taught individuals to count only on themselves instead of teaching them to expect everything from the crippled Providence of government, if they had sought to produce money-makers instead of pushing the masses to the sterility of controversy and the shame of begging, liberty which, whatever the sophists may say about it, is a matter of dollars; happiness which, whatever the lazy say about it, is a question of morality and work, would be instituted universally in France, and the government, neglected in its corner, would concern us little. A people which goes about its business is a people which governs itself, and a people which governs itself abrogates, by this single fact, and renders obsolete the whole legislative morass, the conception of which was favored far more by popular agitation than the genius of statesmen.

After having indicated what, in my conviction, is the truth, i.e.: that the governmental institution, worn out, decrepit and corrupt in 1848, carried along as it was by events and the flux of interests, would gradually and forever have vanished, if the inopportune popular movement hadn't raised it back up and rejuvenated it; it remains for me to demonstrate how this movement, governmental as it was, might have been revolutionary, industrial or anarchic.

IV

On 24 February, at two in the afternoon, the Tuileries, the legislative palace, the ministerial buildings, the Hôtel de Ville, the prefecture of police were all deserted; the official hierarchy was eclipsed; authority had materially vanished, the people was free.

And it should be understood what the word "people" means, when coming from my pen: when I use this word, I'm referring to everyone, shirts and clothes, polished boots and hobnail shoes.

On 24 February, I say, the people was free, that is, nobody had more or less authority than anyone else, everyone had the same authority; and when the authority of everyone is equal to that of all, social equilibrium has necessarily been attained.

This is a mathematical certainty and natively simple: everyone can see the neutralization of forces by their parity; consequently, everyone sees how, in a group of men who are equally invested with the faculty of subjection, liberty finds a footing. If what I can do to you is the same as what you can do to me, our mutual respect is assured: we are at peace.

This was the State of both Paris and France on 24 February 1848.

The Revolution was brought about. However, the revolutionary movement was a mistake; a mistake for which the people would pay dearly if this movement hadn't succeeded; a mistake for which the people pays very dearly ever since this movement, which only succeeded in an artificial manner, turns out to have consolidated the very thing that would have been destroyed by interests: the tutelage.

The movement of February 1848 was a mistake because, on one hand, the public needs pursued the abrogation of the tutelage, and because, on the other hand, every street movement, as a mutiny, demands and, consequently, confirms said tutelage. I can't accept that an armed action can be successful without discipline; and there is no discipline without a leader, no leader, either, without subordinates. The movement of February, like that of 1830, was an armed action, it therefore had its leaders, its guardians; in other words, its necessary and inevitable government, but it's precisely against the government, not of Charles X, not of Louis-Philippe, but of anyone at all, it's against government in principle that interests militate, that Revolution struggles; the movement of February, which bore the government in its womb, wasn't in step with either the interests or the Revolution: which means that it was a mistake.

But why did this movement satisfy the Revolution for a moment? It's because, before this manifestation, the government, which is neither at the Tuileries, nor at the Hôtel de Ville, nor at the Elysée, but which is found in the interests, which inform public opinion, was already condemned by public opinion: this is because, before it was accomplished by the movement, the Revolution had been made by the interests, which is called faith by the doctrinaires.

But, between the genius of the interests or faith and that of the movement, there was an essential difference that would soon be translated into a misunderstanding: the industrial force targeted the institutions, the faith separated itself from authority; the movement targeted men only. We all know in what a striking manner the interests have protested against the movement and its results. Let us say what could have been done to assimilate the movement with the Revolution.

V

The fact of the revolution was accomplished.

Antagonisms, these deformed children of the governments, were effaced in the heart of the Republic, which truly was the Republic, since it had no godparents.

Fairness, this supreme justice of the people, hovered alone above the City, taking the place of the law that it had just abrogated.

The bank and the palace of finance had the unusual good fortune of seeing Liberty keep watch at their door, and they had no complaints.

Theft, which had been warned by the improvised inscriptions on the prompt fate that was reserved for it, was punished by death that very hour. Theft, besides, only exists in the state of privilege; free competition radically erases it.

The parties, these vermin that emerged from the decay of the courts, both high and low, had vanished along with the cause that produces them.

The complete forgetting of the past had brought all the citizens together.

The Fraternity was universal.

The most heartfelt courtesies were exchanged in the streets, in the public square.

Joy and hope lit up all faces.

Everyone, no longer defended by anyone but himself, sought a support in everyone and easily found, in this sense of isolation, the reason for the respect he owed to others.

The most perfect order reigned everywhere at the same time as the mob.

No one was afraid, for everyone was king.

Since no one was afraid, confidence was generalized.

I consider this picture of the public situation on 24 February 1848 perfectly accurate. I assume that the population of Paris would have set, in the foreground of this stage, a simple urban or municipal commission and a magistrate who, with his face towards the border, was especially concerned with sending word abroad, and the new state of France and its peaceful attitude in this hypothesis, I affirm this, but I'll demonstrate it soon, the result of the movement remained conformant to the demands of the Revolution, sovereignty stayed put, liberty was gained and domestic tranquility assured.

What else could really be asked for? A ministry of the interior? But this would bring individual and municipal liberties into question once more, and reconstitute a tyranny and a budget, the abolition of which was pursued by the interests.

A department of education? But this would bring academic freedom into question, and reconstitute a tyranny and a budget, the abolition of which was pursued by the interests.

A department of religion? But this would bring freedom of conscience into question, and reconstitute a tyranny and a budget, the abolition of which was pursued by the interests.

A department of trade? But this would bring into question the freedom of transactions, and reconstitute a tyranny and a budget, the abolition of which was pursued by the interests.

A department of agriculture? But this would bring into question the freedom of land property and reconstitute a tyranny and a budget, the abolition of which was pursued by the interests.

A ministry of public works? But this would bring into question the freedom of private enterprise and reconstitute the communism of State works and a tyranny, the abolition of which was pursued by the interests.

A department of finance? But this would bring into question the freedom of credit and reconstitute a monopoly and a budget, the abolition of which was pursued by the interests.

A department of justice? But this would bring into question the justice of juries and reconstitute the political jurisdictions and a budget, the abolition of which was pursued by the interests.

A police prefecture? But this would bring into question the sovereignty of the municipalities, again bringing in a State police to replace their own police, and reconstitute a tyranny and a budget, the abolition of which was pursued by the interests.

A department of war and a department of the navy? So be it. These offices are the natural annexes of foreign affairs, and those who work in them are commissioned by the head of the chancellery designated above; the people had nothing to worry about here, beyond the accounting that would have keep a record of the least receipts and the slight expenses called for by this small administration.

A municipality and a chancellery: these should, therefore, and would have been the official face of the government of the people, if so many climbers, scorning the democratic condition of simple citizens, hadn't stubbornly aspired to be made ministers; prefects, sub-prefects, receivers, inspectors, etc., etc. Democracy doesn't consist in having all the municipalities governed by one municipality, all individuals by one or many individuals, it consists in leaving each municipality and each individual to govern themselves on their own responsibility. But, with respect to the mayor and the municipal council, the individual governs himself; for it never occurs to a municipal assembly, which has no prefect's support, to control the business and occupational interests of the citizens who elected it. Tyranny comes from communistic or monarchical centralization; individual liberty is found in the municipality; the municipality is essentially democratic. Nothing should be placed above it, without bringing the monarchy back.

Just as the individual governs himself with respect to the mayor, likewise, with respect to the chancellery or diplomatic administration, the municipality or the complex individual, governs itself; for it would never occur to one whose only task is to represent the nation to the foreigner, to meddle in municipal affairs.

The tyranny comes from the monopolization by the State of the domestic elements of society; the communal liberty is secured when the central authority has only a purely diplomatic character and attributions free from any infringement on the prerogatives of individuals; for everything that happens in the interior should be carried out by the people itself, by private individuals; things that are physically impossible for the people to do by itself, i.e., by each of its members, things like international acts, peace treaties or trade agreements. These are cases where the need for delegation is evident. This is why only the magistracy that had, in terms of the revolution, the right to spring out of the movement of 24 February 1848, was the external magistracy.

VI

But what? A municipality and a chancellery as the whole government, seemed, to the great revolutionaries, the friends of the people, institutions too unwise and, above all, too peaceful.

How could citizen Ledru-Rollin have brought back the royalists that he wanted as opponents, if he hadn't recalled them by taking Duchâtel's place? Ledru-Rollin is the author of Baroche.

How would citizen Garnier-Pagès have suffocated the confidence that was just then being born, if he hadn't reopened the ministry of finances and thundered out a new tax? Garnier-Pagès is the author of Fould.

Or would citizen Carnot have been defeated by the Jesuits, if he hadn't been helped by the university? Carnot is the author of Falloux.

How would citizen Crémieux have preserved the magistracy of the monarchies, if he hadn't been installed in the justice department? Crémieux is the author of Rouher.

Would the State's inquisition not be dead if citizen Caussidière hadn't become the prefect of the police? Caussidière is the author of Carlier.

Far stranger things would have happened, if citizen Louis Blanc, the Ignatius of socialism, hadn't preached the crusade of labor against capital every single day; Louis Blanc is the author of Montalembert.

All those republicans who, as such, should have a blind confidence in the public's common sense, started by distrusting the public's good sense, which was so republican that even the republicans paled beside it.

In the presence of universal republicanism, the *National* didn't know what to do with itself, and the *La Réforme* was threatened with asphyxiation. After the disappearance of authority, since each citizen had an interest in sparing everyone else, there was no more animosity in the country: since politics had fled along with the government, the question became entirely economic, numbers replaced controversy.

But the doctrinaires didn't find any benefit in this; they were keenly aware that, from the moment when everyone begins to look after their own business, the business of the whole would fare quite well; but then, anyone else could do as much as them, and they would find themselves forced to work like anyone else; then, there wouldn't have been any parties, and the agitation that brings a living to vagabonds and statesmen would cease; then, politics would vanish, and those who live without doing anything would have nothing more to do. Hence, the necessity of rescuing the government.

But how to approach it? The Government's only mission is to bring people together in agreement; and everyone was in agreement. No government was possible, and yet a government was called for; one was required. Democracy had its staff like the royalty; like the royalty, it had men whose devotion to the fatherland went as far as to occupy the kitchens and the ministerial palaces; like the royalty, it had its great citizens who were ready to sacrifice their obscurity to attain a prefecture, at the risk of grabbing 40 or 80 francs a day; like the royalty, it had heroes who were more modest, but no less deserving, capable of renouncing common toil to sit in the sub-prefectures. There was a need, if not for France, which was then quite happy, at least for those who wished to pay it the tribute of living at its expense, for a government. It was necessary, in addition, as a way to save the governmental principle. Not to have rescued the government would have meant accepting a precedent that would have compromised all the governments of Europe, it would have meant stealing from the dynasties' last offshoots any hope of return: and, to take from princes all hope of return meant taking from the republicans any ability of having the princes as opponents, and the republicans can't lose the princes as opponents without ceasing to be republicans.

Thus, the republicans of February were on the road to ruin, absorbed by the universal agreement, when suddenly *le National*, out of breath, hurled this challenge into the arena:

To the republicans of *the day after* by the republicans of *the day before*.

From this moment, the categories were created, discord sang its victory song and the government of the *friends of the people* was established. Thus, to govern, the republicans, like the kings, set out to divide the population. Marrast instituted the order of *the day before* and Lamartine that of the *moderates*; twenty-four hours before, there were only brothers, twenty-four hours later, there were only enemies.

VII

If the Revolution had been properly understood, nobody would have cared about the government; for the Revolution, a stranger to politics, was simply an economic question. The people should have subjected the politicians to the fate it inflicted on malefactors; as a counterweight to the inscription: *death to thieves*, it should have been written on the walls of Paris: *death to the politicians!* Unfortunately, the people didn't yet know, as it knows today, that politics is high knavery.

As for the economic question, every citizen is called to resolve it on their own account; when politics has disappeared, it's interests, it's business that triumphs, and, to look after their own interests and business, nobody needs a minister, everyone is their own government.

Get rid of the dictatorship of the Hôtel de Ville of 25 February, and the people have nothing to do in the street; politics is the only thing keeping people in the street; business brings it immediately back home, for we all live at home.

Now, can you imagine the immense economic movement that would have resulted from the suppression of politics in the aftermath of the barricades? Labor, which is morality *par excellence*, would be revealed in all its forms in capital, and capital, which is intimidated by politics, but which is necessarily attracted by labor, would take a confident leap into industriousness. Nothing is more reassuring that a population which applies itself to production, for nothing is more worthy of interest than a man who is busy making his living. The confidence this man inspires is general, people readily interact with him, they even seek him out to offer him lines of credit, for those who make credit want guarantees, and the first guarantee of a transaction is morality; and, everyone knows that labor and morality are synonyms. The only honest people that are or can be in the world are workers.

And, when I exclude politicians and vagabonds, there is nothing but workers in society; the capitalist, when rid of the political protectorate that deigns to give him 4 percent, is the natural associate of industry which might bring him 10, 15 and 20 percent. When capital and labor adhere to each other without political intermediation which exploits both of them, they understand each other perfectly, for they can't live without each other, they are complementary to each other and if labor can't work without capital, I don't know what capital means without labor.

At the point where liberty found itself on 24 February 1848, there were not, there could not be any but men disposed to mutual aid. Everyone willingly made sacrifices for their neighbor; the creditor extended all the term of his loans; the owner helped the tenant; people shared their dinner with people they barely knew, and if the restoration of the government hadn't cast half of the population into begging in the antechambers, if, disillusioned about politics, the citizens had applied themselves to useful industry, soon each of them, definitively or provisionally, would have found their place and their bread, and the government of all would long since have been founded.

To sum up my thoughts about the movement of February and of the democratic result it might have had, I will say that this movement lacked a man who, like Washington, understood the justice of the public aspirations. The people has no need for men who love it, the people has been far too loved so far; what it wants is to be left alone to love itself. Philanthropy is a factory, the products of which have been more profitable to the entrepreneurs than to the shareholders. To prove this, I will refer only to Thiers, for whom the love of society has brought great dividends, according to those who once knew the luster of his clothes and the smile of his boots.

When I see a man who styles himself a *friend of the people*, the first thing I do is secure what I have in my pockets, and I consider myself very smart to do so.

That said, I return to my subject.

VIII

The Revolution is the emancipation of the individual or it is nothing; it is the end of political and social tutelage or it makes no sense. In this, I should and indeed am in agreement with all men, even with those who are conventionally called reactionaries and who are, after all, only the minors promised to the tutelage of the self-proclaimed democrats, as the latter are today the minors gained for the tutelage of the supposed reactionaries. From the national standpoint, the names of the various parties matter little; all I know here is men, who want to take control of each other, precisely to liberate each from the other. The means are brutal and their inefficacy has been shown by experience; but one certain fact is that the desire for emancipation is everywhere: the Revolution is therefore universal, and this is why, since it refuses localization, that it is the Revolution.

If the Revolution is the end of tutelage, what should the revolutionary logic be?

Will it be political opposition?

Will it be insurrectionary opposition?

Neither politics, nor insurrection, I respond, and I'll prove it:

Politics, in the usual sense of the word, as a social question or a question of the interior, is the art of governing men; it is the consecration of the public minority, the code of tutelage,

tutelage *per se*. To fight politics with politics, to fight the government with the government, is to practiced politics and government, instead of abolishing the tutelage, it only confirms it, it means stopping the Revolution instead of fulfilling it. For, ultimately, what is the opposition, but the critique, in other words, the government of the government?

From the Revolution's perspective, all politics, like all governments, look alike and are equals, for the Revolution is, by principle, by nature, by character and by temperament, the enemy of all politics and of all government, whether social, domestic or of the interior. The Revolution has devoured the *Etats-généraux*, the Constituent Assembly, the Convention, the Directory, the Empire, the Restoration, Louis-Philippe, the provisional government and Cavaignac, just as it will devour Louis Bonaparte and all the guardians who might come later, for the Revolution, I repeat, is the negation of political tutelage.

Politics and the government are not, therefore, nor can they be means to revolution. Robespierre was as hostile to the Revolution as Guizot was; and Ledru-Rollin did no less to stop it than Baroche did; for Robespierre and Ledru-Rollin were politicians, men of government, as much as Guizot and Baroche, from which it follows that, in revolutionary terms, both parties belong to the traditional category of public guardians, which is to be removed. Men who, whether in Parliament, or in the press, bring opposition to politics and to the government, are necessarily anti-revolutionaries, for they are doing politics and government; they are implicated in high political and governmental complicity; they serve the cause of the tutelage and plead against emancipation.

This might seem paradoxical at first, but it's quite true. When an orator from the opposition speaks up against a legal project that infringes on the common rights or liberty, and when the opposition writers take up their pen to combat the governmental measure, they give to this measure, which they can't prevent, the ultimate sanction of adversarial debate; they give it its legal *raison d'être*. To debate is to combat, and whoever combats something has already subscribed to the law which will result from their defeat; and the defeat of the opposition is never in doubt: the government cannot be wrong.

All the legal oppressions, suppressions, prohibitions which have been carried out since the unfortunate invention of the parliamentary regime, are far more due to the opposition than to the governments; I say far more, because there are two reasons why responsibility for these tyrannical measures lies with the opposition: firstly, because it provoked them itself, secondly, because it regularly becomes complicit in their adoption by debating them.

IX

The parliamentary opposition is born of a logical error which human ambition has miserably had a great interest in propagating. Disordered minds, enthusiastic hearts, moved by generosity and, too often as well, by envy which they might not be aware of, have thought and persist in thinking that the Revolution or Liberty could be represented and localized within the confines of the legislature. Right there, as I said above and repeat, is the fatal flaw in the modern mind. Liberty is not a social principle, it is only an individual thing; nobody can represent any liberty but their own personal liberty; the minute a man poses as the representative of the liberty of others, he is already an authority. And the authority of liberty is transformed and suddenly becomes the liberty of the authority; the only free person left, in this case, is the delegate; the magistrate absorbs the city.

Let's also note that, by situating themselves with the parliamentary opposition in the discussion of the acts of power, the writers of the opposition press are playing politics, that is, with power, and that, by imitating the government in taking care to appeal to the country as a guarantee for its acts, they truly displace the country, which is social and not political, which is engaged in industry and business, not controversy.

I will repeat, therefore, having demonstrated it enough by now, that politics is not a means to revolution. The facts, moreover, support my argument. The political history of the past sixty years confirms all that I've said: thanks to politics, the question is the same today as it was on the morning the Bastille was seized.

Now comes the second question, relative to insurrection. I've nearly said, speaking of politics, all there is to say about insurrection. Insurrection is the opposition in the street; here it no longer debates, it acts; it's still the same fight, only it has taken on material dimensions. Win or lose, its triumph or is defeat are summed up in the government, i.e., in the negation of the Revolution.

The insurrectionary opposition turns out to have exactly the same character as the parliamentary opposition, in the sense that it affirms the tutelage instead of denying it, that it denies the Revolution instead of affirming it, only, within the bounds of an assembly, the opposition only confirms the principle of government, while in the street, it confirms the reality of it.

Insurrection is, therefore, no more a means to revolution than politics is, and, here again, the facts support of my argument. It is, indeed, obvious from experience that all insurrection has only served to shore up and even, I might add, to aggravate the tutelage.

So much so that it has become as urgent as it is rational to renounce, in order to fulfill the Revolution, the means, acknowledged as ineffective, of politics and insurrection.

When these means, which are the ultimate resort of these so-called revolutionaries, who would be more appropriately called "ambitionaries", when these have been lost, what will remain? This will be the subject of a final examination.

X

I've said that the Revolution was the substitution of the individual for the traditional State; this definition will make sense to everyone once I've explained what the traditional State is.

The notion of the State, as we have inherited it, invests all the elements of social life in a supreme magistracy, king, emperor, president, committee, assembly. In conformity with this notion, nothing is done, nothing is said, nothing moves in the country but in virtue of the laws emanating from the official person, the reason of the bureaucrat is the reason of State and, from then on, before thinking, before acting, before moving in view of their own welfare, individuals should, act and move in view of the preservation of the magistrate, the cornerstone of the public edifice. This is communism or monarchy, which amount to the same thing.

In this strange combination of a barbaric mechanism, each individual, held in a bridle, guided by the reins and driven by a whip, finds himself harnessed, like a beast of burden, to the car of the State or the supremacy. The State, the universal director, stops or initiates, pulls back or drives forward, at its wishes and according to its whims, art, science, education, religion, industry, trade, credit, without worrying about anything but its own security. The logic of the State, as developed by Rousseau and as practiced by Robespierre, Guizot, Ledru-Rollin, Thiers, and Louis Blanc, admits this enormity, which is that, as long as the supreme magistracy is saved, all Frenchmen could be destroyed without any harm to the health of the State; for the State is this magistracy itself; whoever attacks it attacks the State, and, provided it stays standing, all else can perish around it without any peril to the State.

This is the rational State. Thiers, Cabet, Berryer, Pierre Leroux, de Broglie, Louis Blanc, Laroche-Jaquelein, Considérant know no other. Well, the aim of the Revolution is to detach the individual from the straps of this harness; the aim of the Revolution is to substitute real or individual agency for public or fictive agency. From the traditional perspective, I am led for the profit of my guide; from the revolutionary perspective, I lead myself for my own profit; from the traditional perspective, the magistrate ceases to be an individual by becoming the State; from the revolutionary perspective, the individual becomes the magistrate; the State is the individual.

At to this point in our demonstration, we can cast a decisive light on the flaws in the political and insurrectionary means employed to date.

With the State as a given, when I gather my fellow citizens in a confined space or in a public square, asking them to place their confidence in me, to launch, orally or with arms, combat against the State, the last thing I'm offering is to overthrow the institution for their benefit; I'm simply aiming to substitute my person for the person I wish to fight against; my only goal is to remove those who carry out the direction of public affairs and take it for myself; I may believe that I would direct things better than them, but I am inevitably mistaken; since the point is to get rid of direction altogether: direction, of whatever sort it may be and from wherever it may come, is necessarily a bad thing.

The institution of the State can only be overthrown by the opposite institution. And the opposite of the State is the individual, just as the opposite of fiction is fact. Let the individual be instituted and the State will perish; let liberty be established, and authority will vanish.

But how, it's asked, should liberty be established? How will the individual be instituted?

The individual is instituted when he applying himself to do by himself that which, to date, has been left to the initiative of the State; liberty is founded upon labor, production, wealth and nothing else.

XI

I'm not aware of anything more obscure than the demonstration of evidence, the analysis of a simple notion requires such careful attention that I'd lose heart if I weren't buoyed by the way the public today now pays attention to these questions.

When I speak of the substitution of the individual for the State, I mean to say that the regulatory legislation, by means of which the State has appropriated the direction of public affairs, should be abrogated, and that each individual should start to do their own business, no longer in conformity with the law of the State, but in virtue of their own instincts directed by their own interests.

But nobody can ask the assemblies to abrogate the laws; the abrogation of the State's law cannot be the State's initiative, the State cannot rob itself; this operation returns, by right and in fact, to the initiative of the individuals who invested it in the State.

A State law is abrogated when social realities are placed in opposition to it. All the laws of the police, for example, are abrogated, and all the police agents go away, on the day when the social reality becomes generally and entirely calm.

And the social reality will be generally and completely calm when party opposition, or verbiage, vanishes and allows the physical opposition of the real interests and effective labor, in other words, the popular or individual opposition, to act freely. The laws of the State are powerless against the power of the social needs.

We bring an effective opposition to the police when, without any other concern, we closely pursue our material interests; for, since these interests are the enemies of all disorderly or Statist agitation, it follows that, to pursue them is to cease our agitations; and to cease our agitations means quite simply to do away with the police, unless, which would make no sense, the police has its *raison d'être* in something other than agitation.

When the police force has been absorbed by labor and interests, the suppression of State regulations, the abrogation of the laws proceeds rapidly; for the confidence that brings credit develops quickly.

Everyone look after their own interests; therefore, everyone works; everyone works, therefore nobody threatens anyone, therefore nobody is afraid; nobody is afraid, therefore security is universal.

When security is universal, capital, which had been driven by fear into the caves of the State bank, pokes its peeks through the skylight and, catching sight of industry, who promises it six, ten, fifteen, twenty percent, it naturally asks itself this question: *What am I doing in here?* To this question, capital replies: *Fear of being robbed has imprisoned me in this privilege of making four percent; the outside agitation has ended; I'm no longer afraid and I might get, if I go outside, the double benefit of freedom and a bigger profit: let's go!*

Capital departs from the bank of instinct, and you'll immediately find it liaising with intelligence and industry, to find out what would be best done to realize the greatest benefits; the association of money and labor takes place progressively; the financial monopoly is destroyed by the interests of finance itself: free or individual credit is established. The most beautiful jewel in the State's crown will thus vanish quite gently and without the government having any more right to complain of impoverishment than the police agents had to rail against their own Suppression.

XII

O when, instead of a single storehouse of money, the country possesses, for the sale of this merchandise, as many shops as there are capitalists, metal wares can't fail to be in good shape. Cloth is inexpensive in France thanks to the extension granted to its sale by freedom in its trade! If cloth were monopolized the way money currently is, frocks would become a rare distinction.

Once capital is set free, labor will be activated. Capital and labor are one and the same thing; capital comes from labor and returns to it, or rather, never comes out from it, it moves within it; when labor holds still, capital is paralyzed; labor only walks on the legs of capital, but capital can only think with the head of labor. This duality forms only one body and has only one aim: production.

Those who have said that there was an essential antagonism between capital and labor have only wanted to retain the means of governing both; and to govern is to exploit. By mistrusting both of these officious thirds, capital and labor communicate with each other without a go-between, when they communicate, they know each other and when they know each other, they stick together; for people only go to war because they don't know each other.

Take a close look at society after the suppression of the official opposition, after the determination of political inertia and the calm that resulted, after the disappearance of the

State's police and the conversion of the financial system, and you will notice how quickly the transformation develops.

No more stupid declamations in the press; that abstract quibbling which has never proved anything, which can't prove anything, which has never produced anything but agitation, which can never produce anything but agitation, falls back into obscurity: a people which turns to positivity no longer has time for such quibbling. The public shrugs off this ignorant rabble that can only speak of doctrine because doctrine is like God, like the unknown, like the insoluble: the theme of stupidity and the battle-horse of empty heads.

When the press turns to positivism and industry, like the people, the legislation which disturbs and exploits it has no further *raison d'être*: it finds itself repealed de facto, or in terms of unenforceability, which amounts to the same thing.

When individual liberty is guaranteed, no longer by a scrap of paper but by the far more eloquent reality of generalized security and private confidence; when industrial liberty is guaranteed by the best of all constitutions: that of anarchic or non-regulated credit; when freedom of the press is guaranteed by the strictest of princes: interest; these three fundamental liberties must inevitably, fatally produce all the minute liberties which are presently imprisoned in the boxes of five or six departments. The absorption of the State by individuals will be the work of one year at most; within a few months, the government, stripped of the budget of the interior, of the budget of religion, of the education budget, of the labor budget, of the budgets of industry and trade, of the agricultural budget, and of the budget of the prefecture of police, will find itself, by the force of things and without any thought of crying for help. Reduced purely and simply to the democratic proportions of the department of foreign affairs and its two annexes, one of which is permanent and the other contingent: the navy and war. The government will, ultimately, be, no longer an internal or domestic government but an external or diplomatic government: a chancellery.

As for us, we call this, with or without the permission of our dear revolutionaries, the revolution: for we are the one who wants, in deeds and not words, a revolution that is proper, equitable, and beautiful, a revolution that would be a great thing at the same time as a good thing for the nobleman, for the bourgeois and for the worker, since for the revolution as for God there are neither nobles, nor bourgeois, nor workers, or rather there are only workers, there are only bourgeois, there are only nobles because there are only men and because these men, from the anarchical or free perspective, are impoverished and enriched, they rise and fall, they are ennobled and degraded according to the way luck or ingenuity favors or afflicts them.

XIII

Now let's see, as far as it's possible to indicate, wherein the revolutionary mechanism consists:

Convinced as we are, and as experience and the passage of time have forced us to be, that politics, the new theology, is a base plot, an art of spinning wheels, a strategy of caverns, a school of theft and murder; convinced that every man who pursues politics as a career, whether offensively or defensively, i.e., as part of the government or the opposition, as manager or critic, aims only at seizing other people's property by taxation or confiscation and finds themselves ready to descend to the street, on one side with one's soldiers, on the other with one's fanatics, to murder anyone who would dispute the spoils with him; having attained the knowledge, consequently, that every politician is, unknown to himself, to be sure, but truly, a thief and a murderer; sure as the day that gives its light that every political question is an abstract question, just as insoluble and, therefore, just as idle or stupid as a theological question, we separate ourselves from politics just as eagerly as we would run from the scene of a crime.

Once separated from politics, which had taught him to hate, to envy, to make war upon his fellow citizens, to dream of fleecing them, to negate himself to the point of no longer counting on himself, and waiting for everything from the hand of government, which can never give him anything that it didn't already take from others: once, let's say, he's separated from politics, the individual recovers his self-respect and feels worthy of the confidence of others, his activity, wrested back from the darkness, is unfolded in broad daylight; he leaves the ambush and gets to work.

He is poor and without credit, it will be hard at first, but if he never makes a beginning, how will the marauding ever end? His intentions are good, his actions impressive, his will is firm, he seizes courage with both hands, and suddenly you'll see him chasing an outcome in real society, his natural domain.

He will inevitably find this outcome matched to his merit. It may be that, although he's a skilled clockmaker, initially he only finds work in metalsmithing; it may be that, having a good hand for cabinet-making, he is forced for the moment to work as a joiner; it may be that, as a lawyer, the absence of clients relegates him from the start to study to be a notary, a solicitor or a bailiff; it may be that, as a journalist, his best current bet is teaching in a boarding school or keeping records. What does it matter? All paths can lead to the goal. He creates for himself, whatever position he may be in, relations that he can render amicable. If he really has aptitudes superior to what he's working in, sooner or later he will encounter someone interested in utilizing his talents. He himself possesses the time, activity and discernment necessary to improve his rank. For the moment, he works, therefore he speculates; he speculates, therefore he makes money, he makes money, therefore he owns; he owns, therefore he is free. He institutes himself in principled opposition to the State, by ownership; for the logic of the State strictly excludes individual ownership; in this, the new apostles of the doctrine of the State are far more mathematical than the old ones, and Thiers is but a tiny despot compared to Louis Blanc. He institutes himself, therefore, individually by ownership, his liberty begins with the first dollar, and he will be all the freer in the future when he has more of them. This is the naive and simple truth, the truth of facts, which is self-demonstrating like all light and evidence.

Let rhetoricians call it a monarchy or oligarchy, empire or republic, in whichever State I have dollars in my pocket, I don't care about their arguments. They only draw my attention when, in virtue of some phantasmagoric law of equilibrium, they want to take my dollars from me. Then, let them call themselves monarchists, oligarchs, imperialists or republicans, I know that my vocabulary allows me to give them another, more infinitely more intelligible name and, especially more conclusive: I call them swindlers.

XIV

But is it that authorizes the great swindle of the State? What makes the governments levy an enormous premium on the time, on the work, on the possessions, on the lives, on the blood, of individuals? It's fear. If nobody was afraid in society, the government wouldn't have anyone to protect, and if the government had nobody to protect, it would lose all pretext for the character of its work, of the origin of its possessions; it would no longer be able to call for the sacrifice of the blood or lives of anyone.

When, to speak only of our profession and of all the professions are annoyed like our own, we seek out the reason for all the obstacles placed before us; when we ask why we have to consult the minister, and then the procurer of the Republic, and then also the prefect of police to produce a newspaper, we find that the government is afraid, but we also see that the government is stronger than us, who gives this power to the government? Everyone's money, the public wealth, but if it's a given that the public wealth pays the government to be afraid, it is demonstrated that the public wealth itself is what is afraid.

Why is the public wealth afraid? Precisely because it is what is at stake in all the political or insurrectional politics, precisely because the public wealth which, by nature, is revolutionary or circulating, is incessantly repressed by the governmental piston of agitation and idleness.

The public wealth sustains the government, not for the good it does, this good is seen nowhere and at no time, but for the evil it is thought to stave off. The evil feared by the public wealth and which the government is thought to prevent can only come from the government itself, or from the initiative of those who can bring this or that system into the government; the public wealth therefore sustains a government precisely because it fears another one; it supports the politics of Peter because it's afraid of the politics of Paul. If the Paul-opposition withdraws from politics, the Peter-government is ruined; for, since wealth only supports Peter because he keeps Paul from committing a certain evil, once Paul no longer inspires fear and can no longer commit his crime, when he works instead, the wealth in circulation goes straight to him, Peter loses all support, his actions become null and void, his influence dies, his authority vanishes. Confidence is reborn in all minds, free credit is established, interests are developed to the widest scope, welfare is generalized, prosperity becomes universal, civilization is extended to all the classes, and the Revolution is made.

The complete abandonment of politics, a serious return to business: here, then, is the true revolutionary tactic; it is simple like all that is true, it is easy like all that is simple, and it is simple, true and easy like all that is right.

The government of the people is neither a doctrine nor an idea, it's a fact; this government is summed up by no motto, nor any color, its symbol is a dollar.

THE ELECTORAL LAW

In the first issue of this journal, we have clearly, even audaciously expressed our opinion on the present character of the electoral law. The attitude of the people in reaction to the partial suppression by Parliament of this right has shown us that this doctrine was in keeping with the general sentiment. The electorate is not a principle.

Popular instinct is a surer bet than the reasoning of sophists, for this instinct is connected to reality. The so-called democratic parties can shout all they like about how universal suffrage is the only guarantee of progress, the only principle from which welfare flows, but the facts reply that universal suffrage, the exercise of which has, to date, improved the position of certain elected officials, considerably compromised the interests of private individuals and, consequently, public prosperity.

Does this mean that limited suffrage, as formulated by the majority, will solve the problem? It would be idiotic to suppose so. The truth is not in the election, nothing can come of the election, the election is the government's guarantee, and the government is the cause of the malaise, the solution to the problem lies, therefore, in abstention and not in the election.

The people will end by staying away, just as it will end by refusing the tax, this is inevitable and predetermined. It has entered the path that will lead it there, falling into political skepticism, into doctrinal indifference. When the people no longer believes in anything, then it believes in itself. This final belief settles on an appreciation of reality, when positivism has come to this point, the people escape the realm of interpretations to take on determinate proportions; it begins to fight back, it speculates; it no longer agitates, it saves its money; it ceases to vociferate, it chases enjoyment.

Do you know, from the popular point of view, the meaning of the debates that took place in the Assembly between the majority and the minority about the electoral law? These debates mean that the members of the majority think they can only be re-elected by castrating universal suffrage, and that the members of the minority are convinced that universal suffrage is indispensable for them to remain in place. This is the true meaning of the discussion; but, in fact, what does it mean for the people to attain the majority or the minority? Nothing. Both have clearly proved this and, even if they hadn't proved it in practice, we think we have, in this publication, provided very clear arguments on this point.

Should we really rejoice so much about the electoral regime as to get worked up enough to defend it? What has it produced? Volumes of laws which, for my part, I won't bother reading, what about you?

Certainly, universal suffrage is what led to the assemblies to which we owe all the prohibitions which crush us, would restricted suffrage have led to worse things? We don't presume so. What then does this enthusiasm mean, which we're meant to feel for universal suffrage, when it's shown that the assemblies have only ended by disturbing and ruining us?

The right distrusts a part of the population.

The left distrusts the other part.

For whom are we taken? Whose thing are we? We distrust ourselves, we, on right and left and we withhold our votes: this is the best thing we could do to bring the whites and the reds into agreement, neither of whom wants anything but our money.

This is the reason for the calm that greeted the electoral law. The most naive of the Parisian papers, and the most conceited, *L'Evénement* and *la Presse*, asked the population for calm, and, when calm came, they congratulated themselves for having been obeyed; to hear them, the wisdom of the people is their doing; without them, the agitation would have shattered the pavements and disturbed the city, what a pity.

Calm comes with the current situation. The people has become deeply skeptical, it believes neither the troubadours, nor the elixir peddlers; you can profess a *tender and deep love* for it, you can try to *reassure* it, it cares neither about tenderness nor reassurance, and it asks itself who would be brazen or insane enough to dare place themselves so high as to love it, and who is the sovereign or the schemer who is so far removed from it that he can promise it security.

The times of exploitation by big words are already far gone, the titles no longer fool anyone, devotion has produced its invoices, it's far too expensive. Nobody still believes in the courtly disinterestedness, to the extent that, from the very moment when anyone sets himself apart from other people to command them, legitimate suspicions are raised about him. In such a state, the people no longer have chiefs, equality is starting to appear; when the people has no more chiefs, no further movement is possible, calm is in the air. And calm itself is the Revolution, no longer that of the schemers, but that of everyone, that of interests and of wealth.

The politicians would rather not leave questions of form, however, the question of substance is what agitates the heart of society. The government, the men of the government, the way of making and constituting the government, the antecedents and the doctrines of this or that individual, the preeminence of this or that system, none of these matter much to the people; what matters to it is welfare, and welfare is clearly realizable by none but themselves; it has been shown that this cannot be obtained by delegation, it is an established fact that it is independent of forms. It is, therefore, with complete and good reason that the people is becoming ever more indifferent about the form, in other words, the government, and that it pays attention to the substance, which is nothing but the people itself and its own affairs.

So let it all come, after the electoral law, the decennial presidency, the presidency for life, the empire, the Devil, as long as the good-for-nothings are damned to silence by the prudence of the workers, the form, as elevated as it may be, will be overcome by the substance; the people will devour the government.

The government is not a fact, it's only a fiction. The immutable and eternal fact, is the people. We, for our part, stand with the fact, and bad times are brewing for those who refuse to break with the fiction.

Made in United States
North Haven, CT
17 June 2023